Jean Fritz's Homesick: My Own Story

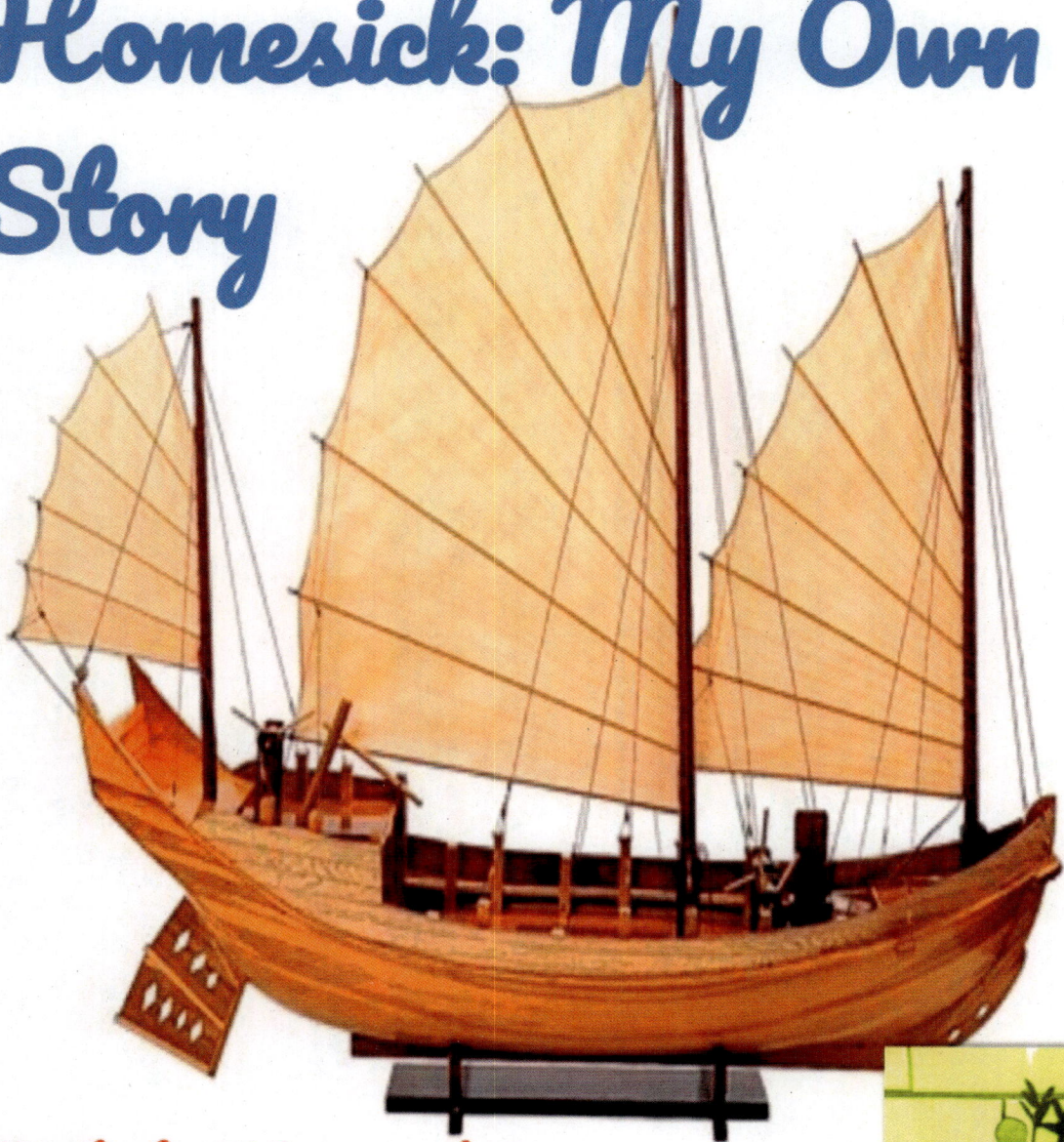

Made by Stones of Erasmus
© 2021

Teacher's Guide and Novel Study for

Homesick: My Own Story by Jean Fritz

By

Greig Roselli

Stones of Erasmus Books

New York, New York

www.stonesoferasmus.com

A CIP catalogue record for this book is available from the Library of Congress.

ISBN: 979-87-1233-3059

Teacher's Manual for Jean Fritz's *Homesick: My Own Story* (Chapters 1-7)

F&P Level: X

Classroom Grade Level: 4 - 6 N.B: Suitable text for middle and high school English Language Learners

Published: 1982

Lexile Level: 860L

Awards: Newbery Honor Book

Table of Contents	
Dedication:	**6**
Note to the Reader	**7**
Pre-Reading	**8**
Pre-Reading Activity - Homesick: My Own Story by Jean Fritz	4
Chapter One	**5**
Word Lists - Homesick: My Own Story by Jean Fritz - Chapter 1	6
Reading Comprehension Questions for Chapter 1	8
Discussion Questions for Chapter One	12
Discussion Group Double Entry Journal	13
Rubric for Reading Comprehension Questions - Chapter 1-7: Homesick: My Own Story	14
Answer Key for Reading Comprehension Questions - Chapter One	15
Discussion Questions Answer Key	20
Chapter Two	**24**
Word List for Chapter Two	25
Reading Comprehension Questions for Chapter Two	26
Extension Activity - Chapter 2 (Homesick: My Own Story)	29
Discussion Questions for Chapter Two	30
Answer Key for Chapter 2 Reading Comprehension Questions	32
Discussion Questions Answer Key	34
Chapter Three	**35**
Word List for Chapter Three	36
Reading Comprehension Questions for Chapter Three	37
Extension Activity: Hankou City Webquest (Chapter Three)	40
Discussion Questions for Chapter 3	42
Answer Key for Chapter 3 Reading Comprehension Questions	43

Discussion Questions Answer Key   44

Chapter Four   **46**
Word List for Chapter 4   47
Reading Comprehension Questions for Chapter 4   48
Going Further: Discussion Questions for Chapter Four   50
Answer Key for Chapter 4 Reading Comprehension Questions   51
Discussion Questions Teacher Guide   53

Chapter Five   **55**
Word List for Chapter 5   56
Reading Comprehension Questions for Chapter Five   57
Discussion Questions for Chapter Five   60
Answer Key for Chapter 5 Reading Comprehension Questions   62
Discussion Questions Answer Key for Chapter 5   65

Chapter Six   **67**
Word List for Chapter Six   68
Geography Activity for Chapter Six   69
Reading Comprehension Questions for Chapter Six   70
Discussion Questions for Chapter Six   72
Answer Key for Chapter 6 Reading Comprehension Questions   73
Discussion Questions Chapter 6 Answer Key   75
Geography Extension Activity Chapter Six Answer Key   78

Chapter Seven   **79**
Characters and Geography List for Chapter 7   80
   Phrases, Unique Terms, and Idioms: 81
Reading Comprehension Questions for Chapter 7   82
Discussion Questions for Chapter 7   84
Answer Key for Chapter 7 Reading Comprehension Questions   85
Teacher Guide for Chapter Seven Discussion Questions   86

Suggested Unit Plan for Homesick: My Own Story by Jean Fritz (Pre-Reading, Chapters 1-7)   **87**
Chapter One Lesson   87
Chapter Two Lesson   90
Chapter Three Lesson   92
Chapter Four Lesson   93
Chapter Five Lesson   94
Chapter Six Lesson   95

Chapter Seven Lesson 96

Go Digital: Google Forms Assessment Links for Each Chapter **98**

Bibliography **99**

Appendix **100**
    Peer Speaking & Listening Evaluation Form 101
    Frayer Model for Vocabulary Instruction 104
    Think About Any Quote! 108
    3-Box Note-taking Template 110
    Cornell Note-taking Template 112

Dedication:

To My English Language Arts Class at Garden

School

In Jackson Heights, Queens

Note to the Reader

The book you are holding in your hand comes from my experience as an English teacher. I was tasked with teaching a group of English Language Learners in the Jackson Heights neighborhood of Queens. Mandarin was their primary language, and they all came to English with varying levels of skill. So — I needed a text that would provide both engagement and textual complexity to meet a wide range of students' skills. I found this Newbery honor book by Jean Fritz. She had lived in China — in a town that one of my students also claims as their hometown. It's called Wuhan today. But it used to be two cities, Hankow and Wuchang, divided by the Yangtze River. So I found my book. And this book is the result of my work with that particular class. It's a charming book. And I think your kids will find Jean's journey to be intriguing. I have designed the book so teachers can use it in their classroom, whether teaching English Language Learners or an elementary or middle school classroom with a mix of different learning styles. I hope you enjoy using this book!

Greig

Pre-Reading

Pre-Reading Activity - Homesick: My Own Story by Jean Fritz

Figure 1: Chinese Junk Keying

The above picture is of the Chinese junk ship Keying. Between 1846 and 1848, The Keying sailed from China around the Cape of Good Hope (the southern tip of Africa) to England. Vessels similar to Keying would have been common on the Yangtze River, where Jean and her family live in Hankow.

- Examine the image closely. What details do you notice about the ship that make it unique?

  The sal,s are sqvared and ruffold

  the boat is coved

  _____

image credit: wikimedia

Chapter One

Word Lists - *Homesick: My Own Story* by Jean Fritz - Chapter 1

Character List:	Geography Terms and Places:
Jean	
Jean's Father (Arthur)	
Jean's Mother (Myrtle)	
Jean's Grandmother	
Miss Williams	
Ian Forbes	Hankow
Vera Sebastian	Yangtze River
	Y.M.C.A.
Andrea Hull	The Bund
Dr. Carhart	Foreign Concessions
Yang Sze-Fu and Wong Sze-Fu	Mud Flats
The Young Boy at the Mud Flats	

Phrases and Idioms:

"God save the King"

"When in Rome do as the Romans do"

"Breathes there the man, with soul so dread / Who never to himself hath said, This is my own, my native land"

Vocabulary Words:

Globe (n.)	Rickety (adj.)
Coolie (n.)	Jaunty (adj.)
Amah (n.)	Recite (v.)
Pagoda (n.)	Sensible (adj.)
Mangled (adj.)	Twinkle (n.)
Consulate (n.)	

Name_____Date_____ Class Period_____

Reading Comprehension Questions for Chapter 1

1. What does Jean's father have in his office?

_____

_____Pg # _____

2. In what city does Jean live? What river flows through the city?

_____

_____Pg # _____

3. Why does Jean feel she belongs on the "other side of the world" when she had lived all her life in China?

_____

_____Pg # _____

4. Why does Jean complain that she cannot run for President of the United States when she grows up?

_____

_____Pg # _____

5. From whom does Jean receive letters from America?

_____Pg # _____

6. Where does Jean's father work? What does he do there?

_____Pg # _____

7. What reason does Jean give Miss Williams for not singing the British National Anthem?

_____

_____Pg # _____

8. At the start of the story, how old is Jean?

_____Pg # _____

9. Who is Jean's friend in China, and why doesn't she see this person often?

_____

_____Pg # _____

10. What deal do Lin Nai Nai and Jean make together?

_____

_____Pg # _____

11. How is Lin Nai Nai different from the other amahs? Why?

_____

_____Pg # _____

12. Why did Jean tell Lin Nai-Nai that American flowers have no centers and "sewing machine" is a greeting?

_____

_____Pg # _____

13. How is Yang Sze-Fu different from other servants?

_____

_____Pg # _____

14. Why does Jean's mother not like it when Yang Sze-Fu makes a butter pagoda for the dinner guests?

_____

_____Pg # _____

15. How does the area of the city around the Bund look different from the rest of the city? Why is this area special?

_____

_____Pg # _____

16. What does Jean do on her way to school?

_____

_____Pg # _____

17. What sign do the British put along the river?

_____

_____Pg # _____

18. How does Jean feel about the Yangtze River?

_____

_____Pg # _____

19. What does Jean carve onto the side of the Chinese junk?

_____Pg # _____

20. On the Bund, who asks Jean why she is not in school. How does Jean respond?

_____Pg # _____

21.   Why does the boy call Jean "foreign devil"?

_____

_____Pg # _____

22.   When Jean says goodbye to the boy by the river what does he say in return?

_____Pg # _____

23.   Why does Jean often get home from school at 4:00 in the afternoon instead of 3:45?

_____Pg # _____

24.   Who is waiting for Jean when she arrives home? What happens?

_____

_____Pg # _____

25.   How does Jean's father solve her problem at school?

_____

_____Pg # _____

26.   Why does Jean go to see Lin Nai Nai after dinner?

_____

_____Pg # _____

Name _____ Date_____ Class Period_____

Discussion Questions for Chapter One

1. Why does Jean sing the British national anthem with her fingers crossed?

2. Jean makes the comment that while her parents tell her, regarding school, "do as the Romans do," she makes the point that her parents do the opposite. They make the Chinese do what the Americans want. How is this evident in the novel?

3. Jean is a child in this story so we have to understand her point of view. What are examples in Chapter 1 of a child's point of view?

4. How does Jean struggle with her identity in Chapter 1?

5. What is Jean's relationship to the city of Hankow?

6. We get to see another side of Jean's imagination when she talks about the Yangtze River and the many ships that pass by the Bund. Why do you think Jean imagines the Chinese Junk is her own ship?

7. What do you think Jeans's motivations are when she stands at the river and says out loud: "Breathes there the man, with soul so dread / Who never to himself hath said, This is my own, my native land"?

8. What is the relationship of Jean to Lin Nai Nai? How does Jean act around her? How are their interactions typical of a nanny and child? How are their interactions different?

9. One prevailing theme that appears in Chapter 1 is not belonging and the human desire to belong. How is not belonging a conflict for Jean? What does Jean do for herself to try to resolve her conflicts?

10. What predictions can you make about how Jean's conflicts will come out in different ways in the novel?

Discussion Group Double Entry Journal

My contributions to our discussion groups:	What I learned from my group:

Additional Notes:

Rubric for Reading Comprehension Questions - Chapter 1-7: *Homesick: My Own Story*

Notes to the teacher:

When grading students' responses to the comprehension questions use the following answer key as a guide. Students should receive credit BOTH for answering questions correctly and providing the correct page number citation. Remind students that answers should be paraphrased or quotes should be integrated into the sentence. Do not accept answers that are copied word-for-word from the text. Also, do not accept answers that are not written in grammatically correct sentences. **Use the following Grading Rubric:**

5 Point Scale Grading Rubric for Reading Comprehension Questions

5 Points	4 Points	3 Points	2 Points	1 Points	0 Points
- Answers are correct and supported with evidence from the text. - Answers are cited with the correct page number(s). - Answers are written in complete, grammatically correct sentences. - Answers include accurate paraphrasing. - Direct quotes are used sparingly and are integrated into the student's answers correctly.	-Answers are correct and supported with evidence from the text. - Answers are cited with correct page - Answers are written in mostly complete, grammatically correct sentences. - Answers sometimes use paraphrases. - Direct quotes are sometimes integrated into the text.	-Answers and page numbers are partially correct and page number citations are accurate. - Answers are partially written. - Answers include a few grammatical errors. -Paraphrasing and direct quotations are not often integrated.	Answers are inaccurate or only include page number citations with one word answers. -Answers are not paraphrased. -Answers rely solely on direct quotations.	Answer only includes page number citation (no written answer).	Answer is not given or not legible.

Answer Key for Reading Comprehension Questions – Chapter One

1. What does Jean's father have in his office? ***Jean's father has a large globe "with all the countries of the world" in his office.***

Pg # ___9___

2. In what city does Jean live? What river flows through the city? ***Jean lives in Hankow. The Yangtze River flows through the city of Hankow.***

Pg # ___9___

3. Why does Jean feel she belongs on the "other side of the world" when she had lived all her life in China? ***She doesn't feel like a real American. She says she belongs in America ("the other side of the world") with her grandparents.***

Pg # ___9___

4. Why does Jean complain that when she grows up she cannot run for President of the United States? ***Since she wasn't born in the United States (she was born in China to American parents) she complains she couldn't run for President.***

Pg # ___9___

5. From whom does Jean receive letters from America? ***Jean receives letters from her grandmother in America.***

Pg # ___9___

6. Where does Jean's father work? What do her mother and father do there? ***Jean's father work at the local Hankow Y.M.C.A. Jean's father is the director and her mother teaches English.***

Pg # ___13___

7. What reason does Jean give Miss Williams for not singing the British National Anthem? ***She says it is not her anthem.***

Pg # ___11___

    8. At the start of the story, how old is Jean? ***Jean is ten years old.***

Pg # ___13___

    9. Who is Jean's friend in China, and why doesn't she see this person often? ***Andrea is Jean's friend, but she lives in the country (and not in the city of Hankow).***

Pg # ___14___

    10. What deal do Lin Nai Nai and Jean make together? ***Jean agrees to teach Lin Nai Nai English while Lin Nai Nai teaches Jean how to embroider.***

Pg # ___14___

    11. Why is Lin Nai Nai different from the other amahs? ***Lin Nai Nai was not born as a servant. She ran away from her husband when he took a second wife and came to Hankow.***

Pg # ___17___

    12. Why did Jean tell Lin Nai-Nai that American flowers have no centers and "sewing machine" is a greeting? Jean is frustrated by her American identity. ***Lin Nai Nai and Jean are "good friends," but Jean admits she is often mean to Lin Nai, so she wrongly tells her that the English word for saying hello is "sewing machine".***

Pg # ___17___

    13. How is Yang Sze-Fu different from other servants? ***He lets his fingernails grow out to show that he is not fit for hard, manual labor. He is also stubborn and smokes cigarettes inside the house (where he is not supposed to).***

Pg # ___18___

    14. Why does Jean's mother not like it when Yang Sze-Fu makes a butter pagoda for the dinner guests? ***Jean's mother thinks serving a butter pagoda to the dinner***

guest is unsanitary because she says Yang Sze-Fu molds it with his own hands and carves it with his fingernails.

Pg # ___19___

15. How does the area of the city around the Bund look different from the rest of the city? Why is this area special? *The area of the city around the Bund (the street that runs along the Yangtze River) is different from the rest of the city because it is mainly occupied by international communities from England, Russia, France, Japan, and Americans. The area is a section of the city completely separate and autonomous with its own rules of extra-territoriality.*

Pg # ___20___

16. What does Jean do on her way to school? *She doesn't go to school; she skips school and instead of attending classes,Chinese government's authority walks along the Yangtze River.*

Pg # ___19___

17. What sign do the British put along the river? *The sign is meant to ban Chinese people from the Bund and it reads "No dogs. No Chinese".*

Pg # ___21___

18. How does Jean feel about the Yangtze River? *Jean has a special connection to the Yangtze River. She mentions it in the beginning of the chapter and explains how much she loves it even though she longs for her home. When Jean walks along the river, she imagines the river is hers and the people populating the Bund her audience. When she she sees the Chinese Junk floating in the river she imagines it is her own ship. She also tries to write poetry about the river and she tries to draw it.*

Pg # ___21-23___

19. What does Jean carve onto the side of the Chinese junk? **She carves her last name in Chinese which is Gau.**

Pg # ___24___

20. On the Bund, who asks Jean why she is not in school. How does Jean respond? **A British Concession police officer, an Indian man with a red turban, stops Jean and asks her why she isn't in school. She explains that she is running an errand.**

Pg # ___22___

21. Why does the boy call Jean "foreign devil"? **The boy calls Jean a foreign devil because he represents the discontent some of the Chinese have about foreigners living in the city. At this point in time, China has undergone change. The dynasties that ruled China for centuries are gone. China is now a Republic but its road to nationhood is fraught with conflict and discord. As the Chinese become more nationalistic they begin to harbor resentment towards the international settlements.**

Pg # ___24-25___

22. When Jean says goodbye to the boy by the river what does he say in return? **He repeats what Jean says to him earlier. He says "American friend".**

Pg # ___25___

23. Why does Jean often get home from school at 4:00 in the afternoon instead of 3:45? **Because sometimes she has to write on the board fifty times "I will not talk in class".**

Pg # ___25___

24. Who is waiting for Jean when she arrives home? What happens? **Lin Nai Nai, Jean's mother, and Miss Williams are waiting for Jean when Jean arrives home at 4:00**

after skipping school. Miss Williams noticed that Jean was not in school and arrives at Jean's house to inquire about her absence. Lin Nai Nai and Jean's mother are very upset that Jean skipped school; but, they are happy she is safe.

Pg # ___26___

25. How does Jean's father solve her problem at school? **Jean's father explains to Jean that the British national anthem and the American national anthem both have the same tune. So to avoid getting into trouble, Jean can simply sing the words of the American anthem "My country tis of thee" and no one will know!**

Pg # ___28___

26. Why does Jean go to see Lin Nai Nai after dinner? **She wants to correct her mistake and tell Lin Nai Nai that the proper way to give a greeting in English is "Good day".**

Pg # ___29___

Discussion Questions Answer Key

1. Why does Jean sing the British national anthem with her fingers crossed? ***She sings the words of the song but she does not believe in what the words say. Jean is very much in conflict with what her American identity means to her. She wants to fit in at school, with her peers, but she feels often like an outsider and since she is still a child (and not an adult) she reacts in a way a child would given a similar situation.***

2. Jean makes the comment that while her parents tell her, regarding school, "do as the Romans do," she makes the point that her parents do the opposite. They make the Chinese do what the Americans want. How is this evident in the novel? ***Jean Fritz, the author, assumes the reader understands how international communities were set up in China in the nineteenth and early twentieth centuries. Hankow, similar to other Chinese cities like Shanghai, Beijing, and Suzhou. Sometimes these areas are called foreign concessions. In these areas, often built along the riverfront, England, France, Germany, Russia, and Japan (among others) carved out areas in the commercial areas of cities that existed outside of the authority of the Chinese government. In this way, the concessions were given the right of extraterritoriality. They existed inside China but they were outside Chinese control. While the United States did not technically have concessions in China at the time Jean and her parents lived in Hankow, Americans often lived in these concessions and enjoyed similar rights and privileges.***

3. Jean is a child in this story so we have to understand her point of view. What are examples in Chapter 1 of a child's

point of view? *There are many examples of Jean's point of view. For example, she takes out her anger on her amah while not understanding why. She runs away from school and does not realize right away why this may upset her parents and amah. She notices that Hankow is divided into factions but she does not completely understand all the reasons why. When she is called a foreign devil she does not understand the full implication of the boy's words.*

4. How does Jean struggle with her identity in Chapter 1? *She's an American emigré - yet she goes to a British school - and she lives with her family and servants in an international settlement in Hankow, China.*

5. What is Jean's relationship to the city of Hankow? *Jean is fascinated by the city. She breaks away from her expected routines and explores the Bund on her own. She is both fascinated by the world she lives in yet she often feels like an outsider looking in.*

6. We get to see another side of Jean's imagination when she talks about the Yangtze River and the many ships that pass by the Bund. Why do you think Jean imagines the Chinese Junk is her own ship? *Jean is fascinated by the ships because they seem powerful to her and they are powerful floating symbols in the river. At the beginning of Chapter 1, Jean notices Chinese women standing at the river to pray to the River Gods. In a similar way, Jean needs her own powerful symbol. Also, the ships also represent the relationship between China and the foreign countries that have settled in its cities. Trade is an important link between Asia, Europe and the United States. Furthermore, it is a ship that separates Jean from home - across the vast Pacific Ocean.*

7. What do you think Jeans's motivations are when she stands at the river and says out loud: "Breathes there the man, with soul so dread / Who never to himself hath said, This is my own, my native land"? **The words come from a poem by Sir Walter Scott entitled "My Native Land". You can share the poem with your students for further enrichment. The main idea is that Jean likes to read and she connects what happens to her in life to art and poetry.**

   My Native Land by Sir Walter Scott

   > Breathes there the man, with soul so dead,
   > Who never to himself hath said,
   > This is my own, my native land!
   > Whose heart hath ne'er within him burn'd,
   > As home his footsteps he hath turn'd
   > From wandering on a foreign strand!
   > If such there breathe, go, mark him well;
   > For him no Minstrel raptures swell;
   > High though his titles, proud his name,
   > Boundless his wealth as wish can claim;
   > Despite those titles, power, and pelf,
   > The wretch, concentred all in self,
   > Living, shall forfeit fair renown,
   > And, doubly dying, shall go down
   > To the vile dust, from whence he sprung,
   > Unwept, unhonour'd, and unsung.

8. What is the relationship of Jean to Lin Nai Nai? How does Jean act around her? How are their interactions typical of a nanny and child? How are their interactions different? **Jean and Lin Nai Nai share common interests and seem to genuinely like each other but they do not talk a lot**

because of the language barrier. Much of what goes on between Lin Nai Nai and Jean is unspoken. Also, there is a power dynamic between Jean and Lin Nai Nai. Lin Nai Nai is a servant and she works for Jean's family. Jean is in her care. It is a transactional relationship but it is interesting to explore how this reality defines their relationship - especially as the novel progresses.

9. One prevailing theme that appears in Chapter 1 is not belonging and the human desire to belong. How is not belonging a conflict for Jean? What does Jean do for herself to resolve her conflicts? *Jean figures out how to sing the national anthem without her teacher noticing she is fake-singing but, at the same time Jean keeps her own sense of national identity. At first she was frustrated and took out her anger on Lin Nai Nai, but by the end of the chapter she has resolved some of her conflicts and is eager to make sure Lin Nai Nai is not humiliated by using the incorrect English words she gave her. She makes amends and redeems herself.*

10. What predictions can you make about how Jean's conflicts will come out in different ways in the novel? *Answers will vary and will mostly depend on students' background knowledge of this time period.*

Chapter Two

Word List for Chapter Two

Character List:	**Place Names, Terms, and Geography:**
"Marjorie"	Bund
Andrea	Y.M.C.A.[1]
David	Communist(s)
Edward	Warlords
Millie (Lee)	

Phrases, Unique Terms, and Idioms:

"Had her heart set on"
"Grown-up talk"
"Be good sweet child and let who will be clever"
St. Nicholas
Middy blouse
French Knot(s)
"To lose face"
Gung-shi[2]
a "pound of butter" present

Vocabulary Words:

Rickshaw (n.)_____	Camomile (n.)_____
Autograph (n.)_____	Pioneer (n.)_____
Clever (adj.)_____	Ordinary (adj.)_____
Posture (n.)_____	Inspect (v.)_____
Lacquer (n.)_____	Crisp (adj.)_____
	Misfortune (n.)_____
	Beggar (n.)_____

---

[1] Young Men's Club of America
[2] Congratulations

Name_____ Date_____ Class Period_____

Reading Comprehension Questions for Chapter Two

1. What does Jean think will make her feel more American?

_____

_____

_____Pg # _____

2. What name does Jean prefer and why does she prefer this name?

_____

_____Pg # _____

3. Has Jean ever celebrated Halloween in the United States?

_____

_____Pg # _____

4. What activities does Jean wish she can do but is not able to do while in China?

_____

_____Pg # _____

5. Who writes their autograph in Jean's book? What is an autograph book?

_____Pg # _____

6. Where does Jean sneak off to for a quick visit? Why? Who does she meet there? What isn't there that was there last time Jean visited?

_____Pg # _____

7. What does Jean ask her mother for Christmas?

_____Pg # _____

8. Why does Jean love going to the Hull's house?

_____

_____Pg # _____

9. Do Andrea's parents get along with each other?

_____

_____Pg # _____

10.   Why do the coolies argue when they arrive at Jean's house?

_____

_____Pg # _____

11.   Which of Andrea's siblings is adopted and why was he
        adopted?

_____Pg # _____

12.   Who do the Hull's invite to their home for the Christmas and
        New Year holiday?

_____

_____Pg # _____

13.   What does David ask Jean to do for him and what does Jean
        agree to do?

_____

_____Pg # _____

14.   What is the Y.M.C.A. and why is it important to the story?

_____Pg # _____

15.   In Hankou how do people often travel long distances?

_____Pg # _____

16.   Why does Andrea put camomile in Jean's hair?

_____Pg # _____

17. Who throws rocks at Andrea and Jean as they walk on the wall? Why?

_____Pg # _____

18. What does Jean send her grandmother for Christmas? What does Jean's grandmother usually send her?

_____

_____Pg # _____

19. When Jean opens her gifts on Christmas day what does she realize about time differences?

_____

_____Pg # _____

20. What gift does Jean give Millie (Lee)?

_____Pg # _____

21. How many guests are expected to arrive at Jean's house for Christmas?

_____Pg # _____

22. What surprises Jean about Mille?

_____

_____Pg # _____

23. While playing hide-and-go-seek where does Millie hide and what chain of events does this cause ?

_____Pg # _____

24. What is the name of Jean's family's hometown in the U.S.?

_____Pg # _____

Extension Activity - Chapter 2 (Homesick: My Own Story)

Jean and her friends play games - as children do. Based on the text, what are the rules of these games? How would you play it? Do some research and record your findings here.

Pioneer	
War	
Uncle Wiggily	
Prisoner's Base	

Research

Source	Summary

Discussion Questions for Chapter Two

1. In the novel, we read several examples of differences between the wealthy international community in the settlement, and the poorer Chinese farmers, servants, and laborers. Jean often makes note of this difference as when her father said to her: "The harder a coolie ran and the heavier his load, the sooner he would die"? Discuss.

2. We learn about Jean's character through the letters she writes to her grandmother in the United States. At the beginning of the chapter, Jean confesses, "I'm not always good. Sometimes I don't even try". What recent events in Jean's life may have prompted this confession? What does Jean mean by "good"?

3. When Jean and Andrea play on the top of the border wall that separates the Chinese farmer's land from the international settlements, what do the girls notice? Who do they see? How does their vantage point high atop the wall serve as a symbol? And of what?

4. When Jean watches the children play in the water she notices that some of the boys are riding on a water buffalo. From what we know of Jean's life so far from the novel, how might her childhood be different from the children she sees?

5. Jean spends her Christmas with Mille, an orphaned girl Jean's friend Andrea's family has invited to their home for Christmas. Jean is fascinated by Millie even before she meets her and even gives her a name - Lee. When Jean finally meets Mille, she is disappointed. What might be the reason for her disappointment?

6. How does this chapter contribute to the overall theme of belonging (and not belonging)?

7. It is mentioned in this chapter that several factions are fighting and attempting to gain influence in the country. In fact, a revolution is brewing - as we will learn more about in Chapter Three. Based on the text - who are the groups and what do they want? (*See Chart*)

Name of Faction	What do they want?
Chinese Government (The Republic)	
Chinese laborers and farmers	
Warlords	
Communist(s)	
Foreigners	

Answer Key for Chapter 2 Reading Comprehension Questions

1. Jeans says she would feel more American if her name were Marjorie (instead of Jean). *Pg # 30.*

2. She prefers the name Marjorie because it sounds American. *Pg # 30.*

3. Jean has never celebrated Halloween (since she was born in China and has never lived in the United States). *Pg # 30.*

4. Jean cannot roller-skate, sled-ride, nor be "wild on Halloween night" because these are American activities that she has not experienced while growing up in China. *Pg # 30.*

5. Andrea, Jean's best friend, writes in her autograph book. An autograph book is a book of blank pages wherein friends and admirers can inscribe their names. *Pg # 30.*

6. Jean sneaks off to visit the Bund, a bustling commercial center in Hankow. She sneaks off to avoid going to school (because she does not want to sing the national anthem; and, she flexes her own tween-style of rebellion. She wanders outside of the international concession and goes to the Mudflats, a poorer area occupied by the Chinese. There she sees the same boy (in Chapter 1) who called her a "foreign devil". The Chinese junk ship is not in the river when Jean visits the Bund. *Pg # 31.*

7. Jean asks her mother if she can officially change her name to Marjorie. *Pg # 31.*

8. She loves going to the Hull's house because she likes the freedom her friend Andrea has and she likes the conversation she has with Andrea and her family. *Pg #s 32-33.*

9. According to Andrea, no, her parents do not get along well, and Andrea fears her parents will get a divorce. *Pg # 33.*

10. They (i.e., the coolies) are arguing over who will be chosen to ride Jean in the rickshaw. *Pg # 33.*

11. David is adopted because Andrea's parents were afraid they would not be able to have children of their own. *Pg # 32 & 34.*

12. The Hulls invite Millie, an orphan from the nearest orphanage, to their home for the Christmas vacation. *Pg # 37.*

13. David asks Jean to help him convince Millie to break into the orphanage office and find out who adopted David. Jean says no because she says it is a crazy idea - but then she agrees (although it is tentative whether or not he will follow through with the idea). *Pg # 39.*

14. The Y.M.C.A. is important to the story because it is where Mr. Hull and Jean's father work (and it is the reason why Jean and her family lives in China). *Pg # 32.*

15. People often hire a coolie, a Chinese laborer, who carries passengers in a rickshaw - a usually covered chair on wheels. *Pg # 33.*

16. Andrea puts camomile in Jean's hair to color it (to bring out highlights in her hair). *Pg # 40.*

17. A group of angry Chinese Farmers converge on the wall and throw rocks (although the wall is eight feet tall so Jean and Andrea do not get hurt). It is suggested that the Communists are organizing the Farmers to revolt against foreigners. Pg # 42-43.

18. Jeans mails her grandmother a doily filled with nothing but French knots. Her grandmother usually sends Jean a handmade petticoat. *Pg # 44-45.*

19. She realizes that because of the time difference when it is Christmas in China, it's Christmas Even in the United States. *Pg # 46.*

20. She gives her a red pencil box. *Pg # 44.*

21. Eleven (11) guests are invited. *Pg # 45.*

22. Jean is surprised that Millie is so taciturn and does not seem very happy. *Pg # 47.*

23. Millie hides in the Hull's car (because apparently she wants to return to the orphanage). This causes a commotion and the Hulls quickly leave. when Jean finds out they have already gone and

Jean feels bitter because she did not want the Hull family to leave. *Pg # 49-50.*

24. Washington, P.A. The town of Washington is in Pennsylvania. Jean mentions that her parents refer to the town as Washington, P.A. *Pg # 51.*

Discussion Questions Answer Key

1. Answers will vary but definitely point out the alarming contrasts between the coolies and Jean's family. You may want to ask the students who they sympathize with more and why?

2. Answers will vary but have students share their own stories of growing up. When was that time when you realized that you did not have to follow what your parents told you to do? Guide students to think about Jean's "rebellion" and the larger picture of the novel.

3. The description of Jean and Andrea on the wall in this chapter is very visual. Help students to visualize it by reading the passage aloud. It reminds me of another autobiographical novel - *Empire of the Sun* - (about World War II - but also in China and inside the International Settlement of Shanghai - but about a boy instead of a girl!)

4. This question is similar to question 3. Again - help students visualize the scene by re-reading the passage aloud - show students a photograph of a water buffalo - if they don't know what one looks like.

5. How does this scene show how truly young Jean is in the novel. She's only ten. You can talk about how sometimes our expectations are different from what really happens; Also explore how Millie is treated. Is it really fair to her to be invited to the family dinner just because she is an orphan. This question can be deep. And it also taps into some of the psychology of adoption.

6. This question is a great essay style question if you want your students to submit writing to you!

7. I recommend guiding students through this question and citing textual evidence from the book that describes each group. This question can grow into a project - students can create posters for each group.

Chapter Three

Word List for Chapter Three

Character List:

Arthur Hull

Dr. Carhart

Mrs. Jordan

Kurry

Miriam

Two Catholic priests from New Jersey

The resort mountain town Jean goes to in this chapter is east of Hankou and near the Yangtze River in the Lushan Mountains.

Map: China CIA map

Vocabulary Words:

Revolution (n.)	Enamel (adj.)
Strikes (n.)	Numb (adj.)
Agitator (n.)	Grunt (v.)
Haranguing (v.)	Bluebells (n.)

Place Names, Proper Names, Terms, and Geography:

Peitaiho

Peking (Beijing)

Kuling

Shanghai

Kiukiang

Rattling Brook

Cave of the Immortals in the West Valley

Rain Gods

Phrases, Unique Terms, and Idioms:

Bobbing one's hair

Grape nuts

ke-ren[3]

Mei mei[4]

Bobbsey Twins

---

[3] Friend
[4] Little sister

Name_____ Date_____ Class Period_____

Reading Comprehension Questions for Chapter Three

1. Explain the reasons that the revolution has started?

_____

_____Pg # _____

2. What does Lin-Nai say about how society will change for the rich and poor in China? Who might have influenced her answers?

_____

_____Pg # _____

3. Why is Jean's father worried about the agitator who demonstrates in front of the Y.M.C.A?

_____

_____Pg # _____

4. On the night the riot alarm rings in Jean's neighborhood, what is the reason Jean's mother wants her to do as she says and not ask any questions?

_____

_____Pg # _____

5. What's Jean's father's responsibility in the event of a riot?

_____Pg # _____

6. How does Andrea boast about her new house in Shanghai?

_____Pg # _____

7. How does Jean react when she finds out her family's vacation plans have changed?

_____

_____ Pg # _____

8. What does Jean imagine while Dr. Carhart gives his sermon?

_____

_____ Pg # _____

9. Why is Jean skeptical of Dr. Carhart's analogy?

_____

_____

_____ Pg # _____

10. What are the consequences of Jean leaving Hankou before the Summer holidays begin?

_____

_____ Pg # _____

11. When Jean and her family go to the mountains in Kuling, is Jean afraid? Why, or why not?

_____ Pg # _____

_____

12. Who joins Jean and her family on their trip up the mountain to the Kuling resort village?

_____

_____ Pg # _____

13. What does Jean find in her room that makes her feel at home?

_____ Pg # _____

_____

14.   What does Mrs. Jordan tell Jean after she visits Rattling Brook?

_____

_____Pg # _____

15.   Why does Jean's mother visit the hospital?

_____

_____Pg # _____

16.   Who is Miriam and how does Jean react to her? What does Lin Nai Nai call her?

_____

_____Pg # _____

17.   What does the written note say that the servants give to Jean's father?

_____Pg # _____

18.   What causes Jean to be angry with Dr. Carhart?

_____

_____Pg # _____

Extension Activity: Hankou City Webquest (Chapter Three)

Hankou was an important industrial city on the Yangtze River. The area is divided by the river, with Hankou on the western bank of the river, and the city of Wuchang on the eastern bank. Today the two cities are combined and it is now named Wuhan. Complete the following web quest to learn more about Hankou, both how Jean would have known it in her time, and how it is today.

Website	Task	Your Response
Map of Hankou (1974) <https://www.loc.gov/item/75690968>	Who created this map? Where would Jean have lived?	
Historical Photograph of Hankou <https://www.loc.gov/resource/cph.3c21747/>	What is going on in this picture? Where is this picture taken?	

Study the map (see next page). Colored areas are the sites of the international settlements in the city.

Questions

1. How many rivers flow through the city and what are their names?

2. Which settlement would have been home to Jean and her family? What color is it?

3. How many "cities" make up this region?
4. Which city has already started a revolution?

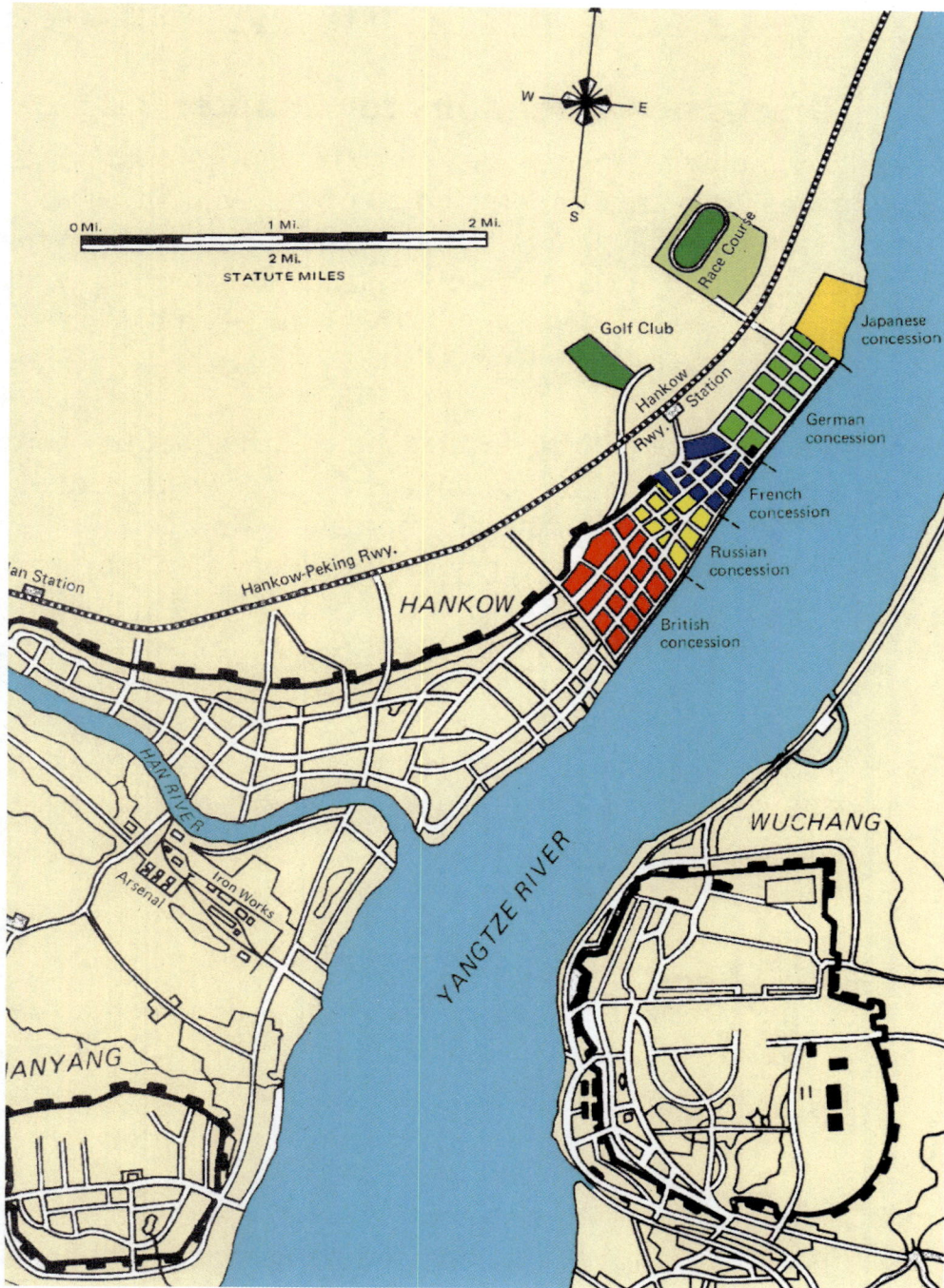

Map credit: Phil Abbey © 1999

Discussion Questions for Chapter 3

1. Jean and her family are in danger - living in Hankou during the revolution. Jean does not understand all of the events that are occurring - and she only learns bits and pieces of news from her father, mother, and Lin Nai Nai. How is Jean's perspective typically a child's perspective? How does Jean witness the events differently from the adults around her?

2. Jean sounds like a spoiled child when she is upset that her parents will not take her to her favorite vacation spot - especially considering how the city has fallen under a state of emergency. How can we sympathize with Jean's immaturity? Is it appropriate? Why or why not?

3. How is Jean's stay in the mountains different from her life in the city?

4. Many of the foreigners in Hankou, including people like Dr. Carhart, Jean's family, Miss Williams, continue to live in China, but follow their own customs and traditions. How do the riots, demonstrations, and protests reflect this?

5. The events of Chapter Three end on a very sad note. What do you think is the effect of this ending on Jean? What do you imagine are the feelings of everyone present? Jean's mother and Father, Jean herself, Lin Nai Nai, and the Jordans?

6. Despite his grief, Jean's father comforts her at the end of Chapter Three. What do we learn about Jean and her father's relationship at this point in the story?

Answer Key for Chapter 3 Reading Comprehension Questions

1. Students, workers, and coolies are protesting and striking. The Chinese are unhappy about the infiltration of foreigners in China. Pg#__53__

2. Lin Nai Nai says that the protesters want a new government in China where the money will be divided equally and there no longer will be rich or poor. Pg#__53__

3. The agitator assembles a group of protesters in front of the YMCA where Jean's father works. They cry that foreigners shouldn't run the place and they threaten to run him out of town. Pg#__53__

4. Jean's mother is afraid that a "mob might burst into the house" and she wants to make sure Jean is safe. Pg#__53-54__

5. Jean's father signed up as an emergency relief volunteer for the neighborhood. Pg#__54__

6. She boasts that her new house will be bigger and outfitted with "five new modern bathrooms" and she will be able to take ballet dance lessons "From an Austrian dance instructor named Hans". Pg#__56__

7. Jean is upset because she wanted to go to the ocean in Peitaiho because it makes her feel free. Pg#__57__

8. Jean imagines climbing the rafters of the church's ceiling, shinnying "up one of those columns". Pg#__60__

9. Jean is skeptical of Dr. Carhart's analogy that life after is death is similar to going through a dark train tunnel. At the end, the train "bursts out of the tunnel into a blaze of light". Pg#__60__

10. She will miss the last quarter of school and therefore unable to receive a complete report card. Pg#__61__

11. Jean is afraid because the journey to Kuling involves going up a mountain in a rickshaw. Pg#__62__

12. Jean is joined by a group of priests from New Jersey. Pg#__62__

13. Jean finds a cat (Whom she names Kurry), old copies of *St. Nicholas* magazine, and a copy of the Bobbsey Twins. Pg#__66__
14. Mrs. Jordan tells her that Jean's mother is in the hospital. Pg#__67__
15. Jean's mother visits the hospital because she is pregnant. Pg#__68-69__
16. Miriam is Jean's younger baby sister. Jean seems both excited and anxious about the news of Miriam. Lin Nai Nai calls her Mei Mei, the Chinese word for "little sister". Pg#__73__
17. The note delivers the news that Miriam has died suddenly and that Jean's father must go to the hospital to tend to his wife. Pg#__74__
18. Since Miriam has died Jean is angry at Dr. Carhart because of the remarks he made in his sermon about death and the afterlife. Pg#__75__

Discussion Questions Answer Key

1. In this chapter, Jean acts selfishly since she can only think about how the disruptions will affect her Summer vacation plans. She is also jealous of her friend Andrea who is moving away to Shanghai. Jean acts like a spoiled child in his chapter. However, Jean is not completely ignorant of the events and what is happening to the city and to China as a whole. Students may want to talk about how Jean's privilege as American causes (or creates) her experience.

2. It is easy to relate to Jean since she is only a child. Who wouldn't be upset that Jean's Summer vacation plans are spoiled? However, direct students to the question of who, in fact, is immature in this story? It is easy to relate to Jean's immaturity since she is just a kid. However, what about the whole international community in Hankou? How are they immature?

3. The atmosphere of Kuling is starkly different from the bustling, chaotic city life of Hankou. Kuling is a resort village created solely for the enjoyment of its visitors. It is physically separate from the chaos going on politically in China and it is also a relief for Jean and her family. Remind students of who is staying in Kuiling. Who benefits from its luxury?

4. Note: This chapter highlights the uncomfortable truth that Jean and her family are occupiers in China. The international settlement is separate from the rest of the city and it follows its own rules, has its own government, schools, and police force. The Chinese are not allowed to live there.

5. Answers will vary. However, it is important to note how Jean's family copes with Miriam's death. This question may bring up personal feelings among your students, especially those who may have experienced the death of a sibling.

6. Answers will vary. The point of this question is to generate ideas about parenting. How is Jean's father good at parenting Jean?

Chapter Four

Name_____ Date_____ Class Period_____

Word List for Chapter 4

<table>
<tr><td>

Character List:

Jean's Father

Jean's Mother

Kurry

Dr. Carhart

Yang Sze-Fu

Blanche

Mr. and Mrs. Gale

Mrs. Little

Nancy

Lin Nai-Nai

Lin Nai-Nai's Little Brother ("Dee-Dee")

Mr. Hu
</td><td>

Place Names, Proper Names, Terms, and Geography:

Places

Hankow

Wuchang

Washington, P.A.

The Bund

Names and Terms

Bluebells and Tiger Lilies

Dodge Sedan

The *President Taft*

Unique Terms and Figures of Speech

"The Narrow Squeaks"

Giddyap

"Napoleon's Last Charge"

Whiz-bang

flapper
</td></tr>
</table>

Vocabulary Words:

Procession (n.)_____ Disgrace (v.)_____
Gangplank (n.)_____ Siege (n.)_____
Storm (v.)_____ Appreciation (n.)_____
Pockmarked (adj.)_____ Steward (n.)_____

Name_____ Date_____ Class Period_____

Reading Comprehension Questions for Chapter 4

1. Why does Jean's father urge his family to return to Hankow earlier than expected?

_____

_____Pg. # _____

2. How does Jean and her family escape the angry coolies?

_____

_____Pg. # _____

3. Why won't Jean return to school in the Fall?

_____

_____Pg. # _____

4. Where does Lin Nai-Nai's family live?
_____Pg. # _____

5. Why does Yang Sze-Fu cut his nails?

_____

_____Pg. # _____

6. What gift does Jean buy for Lin Nai-Nai's little brother?
_____Pg. # _____

7. What does Yang Sze-Fu mean when he tells Jean, "a cat is just a cat"?

_____

_____Pg. # _____

8. How does Jean imagine that Yang Sze-fu is plotting to kill her and her family? What changes her mind?

_____

_____Pg. # _____

9. What is the name of the ship that will take Jean and her family to the United States?

_____Pg. # _____

10.   How does Jean celebrate the end of the siege? What does Jean's father estimate is the number of civilian casualties and sick in Wuchang?

_____

_____Pg. # _____

11.   What happens to Lin Nai-Nai when she goes to find her family?

_____

_____Pg. # _____

12.   How does Jean surprise her mother while talking with Nancy Little?

_____Pg. # _____

13.   What does Jean receive for her voyage back to America?

_____Pg. # _____

Going Further: Discussion Questions for Chapter Four

1. What are the effects of the siege on Jean? On her father and mother? On Lin Nai-Nai? On Yang Sze-Fu? On the people of Hankow and Wuchang?
2. Why do you think Lin Nai-Nai's father refuses to see her? How does war tragically divide both country and family?
3. Once Jean returns to America, do you think she will continue to stay in contact with Lin-Nai? Why or why not?
4. List and explain ways Jean and her family cope during the siege of Wuchang.
5. Even in the midst of a conflict between the Chinese Nationalists and the Communists, how are Jean and her family privileged in this story? How are they both involved in the events of the siege, but also set apart from the conflict?

Notes:

_____

_____

_____

Answer Key for Chapter 4 Reading Comprehension Questions

1. The steamboats on the river might stop running, thus potentially stranding Jean, Kurry, and her Mother in Kuling. **Pg. # 77**

2. After taking charge of their luggage in Hankow's harbor, a band of coolies demand more than double the pay for transport. Jean's father appeases the coolies by paying for what they ask (and more). **Pg. # 79-80**

3. Jean's British school isn't re-opening and Jean's teacher is returning to England. Jean's mother proposes to homeschool Jean. **Pg. # 82**

4. On the other side of the Yangtze River in Wuchang (which has been laid under siege by the Communist army in Hankow). **Pg. # 83**

5. He is now a Communist and to show solidarity he has cut the long nail on his pinky finger to show he is no better than anyone else. N.B. Later in the chapter, he suggests that he misses his nails and Jean feels sorry for him. **Pg. # 82**

6. Jean's family prepares food to send to Lin Nai Nai's family across the Yangtze river in Wuchang. Jean gives Lin Nai-Nai's brother ("Dee-Dee") "a big bar of milk chocolate". **Pg. # 89**

7. He expresses the idea that unlike people, there are "no foreign cats, no Chinese cats, no Communist cats, no capitalist cats. Just cats." **Pg. # 86**

8. Jean lets her imagination run wild and suspects that Yang Sze-Fu is planning to poison her and her family with potassium. She decides not to worry about it anymore when she notices Yang Sze-Fu feeding and petting her cat, Kurry. **N.B.** *Students can infer that if Yang Sze-Fu takes care of her cat and treats it kindly then he is probably not a threat.*

Also, talk to students about the complexity of this conflict. What does it say about Jean's implicit biases? It is a good opportunity to discuss how assumptions about others, their allegiances, their race, ethnicity, and so on, can lead to misunderstandings, and prejudice. **Pg. # <u>84-85; 86</u>**

9. The *President Taft* **Pg. # <u>90</u>**

10. Jean's mother declares a school holiday. Lin Nai-Nai and Jean go to the market for fresh food for the baskets Lin Nai-Nai plans to send to her family in Wuchang. Jean's father estimates many dead in Wuchang (he counts sixty bodies an hour carried in wheelbarrows). About fifty-thousand (50,000) sick will have to be transported to Hankow for treatment. **Pg. # <u>92-93</u>**

11. Lin Nai-Nai reminds Jean's parents that they promised to help her bring supplies to her family in Wuchang once the siege was over. Lin Nai-Nai goes across the river and makes arrangements with Jean's father to send a message from the Y.M.C.A. when she is ready to return to Hankow. However, Jean discovers Lin Nai-Nai has returned prematurely. Lin Nai-Nai explains her father refused the food and would not allow her to see her mother (who was sick). She finds out her older brother has died and her sisters are married and living in Shanghai. She did see her younger brother ("Dee-Dee") who naively promises she can live with him once he grows older. N.B. *Students may also mention that Lin Nai-Nai walked alone (with her bound feet) back to the river and rented a sampan to take her to Hankow.* **Pg. # <u>93-94; 96-97</u>**

12. Jean off-handedly tells Nancy Little that her sister Mirriam, if she had lived, would be four months old. Jean also tells her mother this fact and her mother reacts as if "slapped in the face". Jean's mother does not want to talk about Mirriam. *N.B. Students can infer that it is probably too*

painful a topic for Jean's mother. Jean, since she is still young, does not understand fully the loss of losing a child.
Pg. # <u>95</u>

13. Her father gives her a special blanket, "a steamer rug made especially for ocean voyages". Her grandmother sends her a petticoat and a 1927 calendar. **Pg. # <u>98</u>**

Discussion Questions Teacher Guide

1. Students can talk about what it would be like to live during a siege. Explain to students that Jean and her family are in Hankow, occupied by the Communist Army. They are not in Wuchang, which has been blocked off from receiving goods and supplies. Her father is working with relief efforts. This obviously takes a mental and physical toll on him, for he sees first-hand the atrocities wrought by the siege (something that Jean is shielded from witnessing). Jean's mother has just lost a child, which must be a tremendous loss for her. She puts her energy into homeschooling Jean. Lin Nai-Nai's family is split in two by the siege and by the two warring political factions. Yang Sze-Fu takes the side of the Communists, but he longs for and misses the old traditions that he has since given up. Also, the people of Hankow and Wuchang have suffered much. Lives have been lost, and after the siege, thousands of people in Wuchang are malnourished and sick.

2. Students' answers may vary. Pride is one answer. Lin Nai-Nai's father may feel ashamed. He may see his daughter as being on the side of the communists. It is a sad part of the story. The conflict has torn families apart. Lin Nai-Nai's life will never be the same again. Students can imagine if their own cities are neighborhoods that were split into two factions. How would that change their everyday lives?

3. The author suggests that Jean will lose contact with Lin Nai-Nai

even though they promise to stay in touch. Answers will vary, but students can talk about what they think and feel about Jean and Lin Nai-Nai's relationship. Make predictions.

4. Jean and her family find many ways to cope. Jean spends time with the servants and gets lost in her imagination. Jean is taught by her mother. Jean memorizes the names of the forty-eight states of the United States. Have students discuss how they might find ways to cope.

5. Jean and her family are Americans. They know that eventually, they will be able to leave Hankow by boat and return to their family home in Pennsylvania. Jean's father is an important figure among the ex-patriots living in Hankow. He helps in efforts to alleviate the suffering of the people. But there is only so much he can do, and at the end of the day, the Americans, and Europeans living in China during this time, are more prosperous and well-off than their Chinese hosts.

Chapter Five

Word List for Chapter 5

Character List:	Place Names, Proper Names, Terms, and Geography:
Jean's Father	Hankow
Jean's Mother (Myrtle)	Shanghai
Yang Sze-Fu	Yangtze River
	"The Charleston"
Lin Nai-Nai	Flapper
Mr. and Mrs. T.K. Hu	Victrola
The Hulls and the Littles	Cablegram
The Boy from the Bund	*The Phantom of the Opera* & *Rin Tin Tin*

Vocabulary Words:

Concession (n.; as referring to land or property)

Fad (n.)

Bedraggled (adj.)

Name_____ Date_____ Class Period_____

Reading Comprehension Questions for Chapter Five

1. How are the warring Communist and Nationalist factions alike? How are they different?

_____

_____Pg # _____

2. What specific group took over and occupied the British concession in Hankow?

_____Pg # _____

3. In what ways does the gift of the ginger jar, that Mr. and Mrs. Hu give as a remembrance, evoke an emotional response in Jean? How is the jar a symbol of Jean's sojourn in China?

_____

_____Pg # _____

4. To whom does Jean entrust her cat?

_____Pg # _____

5. How does Jean feel about leaving China?

_____

_____Pg # _____

6. What unfortunate news does Jean learn about Andrea and her

family?

_____Pg # _____

7. What popular dance does Andrea tell Jean she has learned? Does every generation have a popular dance? What is the dance craze that characterizes your generation?

_____

_____Pg # _____

8. What does the Nationalist Army do in Nanking that signals alarm bells for Jean and her family? Where do they go?

_____

_____Pg # _____

9. What do Lin Nai Nai and Jean promise to do?

_____Pg # _____

10.   What familiar face does Jean see on the Bund and what do they say to Jean?

_____

_____Pg # _____

11.   What does Jean think all writers ought to wear? Why? Make an inference.

_____

_____Pg # _____

12.   How does Andrea help Jean find a little bit of privacy and relaxation?

_____Pg # _____

13.   How does Jean's mother surprise her?

14. What conflict arises when Jean and Andrea go to see a "moving picture"? How is the conflict resolved?

_____

_____Pg # _____

15. What causes a delay in Jean's father's arrival to Shanghai from Hankow?

_____

_____Pg # _____

16. What did Lin Nai Nai give to Jean as a going away present? Why does Jean say it wasn't just because she missed Lin Nai that she started to cry?

_____

_____Pg # _____

Notes:

_____

_____

_____

_____

_____

_____

Discussion Questions for Chapter Five

1. In Chapter Five, Jean explores her feelings about leaving China and returning to the United States. When she tells her father that she is "mad at the world … the whole world," what does she mean to say?

2. What are some of the details that Jean takes note of on the boat ride from Hankow to Shanghai? Why is it difficult to truly take in all of the atrocities that have transpired during this time of war?

3. How has Jean developed her idea of becoming a writer so far in the novel? What details about Jean's life make her well-suited for this occupation?

4. Even though Jean is an American, she has not lived in the United States. She is ignorant of current fads and fashion that characterize American culture during the novel's historical period. What do her conversations with Andrea and others in this chapter tell us about Jean's identity? About her conflicted feelings of nationalism? Is it possible to inhabit two places at the same time?

5. Jean's father sends his mother a cablegram. Cablegrams

were efficient ways to send short messages quickly to others via undersea telegraph lines. What future technologies does the cablegram predict? How are we more connected via communication than we were in the 1920s?

6. At the end of the chapter, where is Jean? What predictions can you make about what will transpire once she returns to America?

Discussion Notes:

Answer Key for Chapter 5 Reading Comprehension Questions

1. The first part of Chapter One serves as a history lesson. Both the Nationalists and the Communist groups want a better life for Chinese people. But they both treat their enemies similarly, using murder and inhumane practices as a means to gain control of the people. The Nationalists, led by Chiang Kai-Shek, try to influence the many warlords to unify the country while the Communists, who ostensibly have the same goal as the Nationalists, also have their own ideas about what a unified China ought to look like. Also, even within the Nationalists and Communists groups there is division and discord. These warring, divisive factions lead to inevitable civil war in China. **Pg. # 100**

2. Organized Communist workers took over the British concession in Hankow. N.b. It wasn't the Nationalist Army, but a group of laborers. This shows that factions existed even among the populace and not just in terms of military aggression. **Pg. # 100**

3. The gift of the ginger jar is a symbol of Jean's sojourn in China. It is yellow colored yellow and it has inscriptions written in green for good luck and prosperity. Mr. Hu tells Jean to think about and remember her time in China. For Jean, it evokes complex emotions that originate in her conflicted feelings about place and identity. She is American but a significant amount of her upbringing, growth and development, have taken place in China. Students can discuss how moving from one place to another can have both adverse and positive effects. Talk about what places do we truly call home and why. **Pg. # 101**

4. Jean entrusts her cat to Mr. Hu (and by extension to Lin Nai Nai). **Pg. 102**

5. Jean seems resigned to her fate and she attempts to do things

to make her feel content and happy. She says "everything was going well," and she marks the days on her calendar leading up to the date of the ocean liner's departure in Shanghai. **Pp. #** **102-103**

6. Andrea's parents have divorced. Her father lives in an apartment in Shanghai. **Pg. #** **102**

7. Andrea tells Jean she has learned "The Charleston". Typically every generation has a dance that defines that generation. In the 1950s there was the "Doo-Wop" and in the 1980s there was the Moonwalk. There can be more than one dance, of course, and this answer is entirely subjective, based on taste, culture, and upbringing. Students can also talk about why certain preoccupations characterize growing up, regardless of generational differences. See page 116 for a list of songs that Andrea and Jean would dance the Charleston. **Pg. #** **102**

8. The Nationalist Army occupies the city of Nanking, further north on the Yangtze River from Hankow. This causes Jean's father to instruct his family to quickly pack their luggage and leave for Shanghai sooner than they had originally expected. Jean's father stays behind. **Pp.** **103-104**

9. They promise to open the gifts they had given to each other only after Jean has left China and they both are alone. **Pg. #** **105**

10. Jean sees the boy, "her little friend from the Mud Flats" (see Chapter One). He calls her a "foreign devil"; it's unclear whether or not he recognizes her. **Pg. #** **107**

11. Jean thinks all writers wear glasses. Students' responses to this question will vary but it is likely to lead to a discussion about stereotypes. **Pg. #** **111**

12. Once they've arrived in Shanghai, Jean meets up with Andrea (whom she learns has managed to secure tickets on the same

boat to America as Jean). At their lodging, Andrea lets Jean use a private bathroom. Jean takes a long luxurious bath. The girls dance and listen to the Victrola (and old-timey record player). **Pg. # <u>114</u>**

13. Jean's mother has bobbed her hair. N.B. *Students may not know this hairstyle was fashionable in the 1920s.* **Pg. # <u>117</u>**

14. Andrea wants to see *The Phantom of the Opera* (starring Lon Chaney) but Jean is secretly anxious about watching a horror film. Andrea's parents take charge and they end up seeing a kid friendlier film— Rin Tin Tin (and Jean is relieved). **Pg. # <u>118</u>**

15. Upon leaving Hankow, Jean's father's riverboat is caught on a sandbar in the Yangtze River delaying his trip to Shanghai. **Pg. # <u>119</u>**

16. Lin Nai Nai gives Jean an embroidery featuring the mountains of Kuling. Jean's parents think Jean starts to cry because she misses Lin Nai Nai; Lin Nai Nai represents comfort and nurture for Jean; however, the narrator suggests Jean's feelings are more complex and it is a moment in the novel where Jean comes in touch with her complicated emotions about leaving China behind and starting a new life in America. Students can compare the two gifts, the one given by Mr. and Mrs. Hu, and the gift she receives from Lin Nai Nai. **Pg. # <u>120</u>**

Discussion Questions Answer Key for Chapter 5

1. *Answers will vary*. Guide students to consider how Jean fits into both the narrative and historical events of the story. Many things are outside of her control. Students can relate to this feeling of not having control of one's own life (even without living in a war zone or residing in a foreign country). She says she feels like she is in line to get on the ark, but there is not enough for two of a kind. When the events of life overwhelm us, a natural instinct is to blame our environment. To become angry at others, hence, Jean's anger at the world (see pp. 107-108).

2. The boat is crowded with passengers (babies, children, nuns, flappers!, the elderly, and families like Jean's. The boat crew explain that if one hears firing, "throw [yourselves] immediately on the floor" and that bullets can pierce the boat (but not likely). Metal plates have been affixed to the boat's siding to prevent bullets from piercing the interior. If the alarm bell rings three times passengers ought to take their life vest and "hit the deck". At night, passengers cover cabin portholes. Jean hears bullets at night that go "ping, ping, ping". (see pp. 108; 111-112).

3. *Answers will vary. Guide students to think about the relationship between the narrator, an older, wiser Jean, with the younger protagonist, the younger Jean.*

4. *Answers will vary.* Encourage students to share their own stories, if possible, of living in different places, cities, or countries. Most people have something to say about this topic. Go further and ask students how they identify with their own countries. Is pride in one's country important? Why or why not? If appropriate, the teacher can share their own stories of living in a different place, and so on. N.B. Keep the conversation culturally responsive.

5. *Answers will vary*. Students can talk about the different forms of communication that have arisen since the mid-nineteenth century, including the telephone, radio, television, The World Wide WEb, electronic mail (e-mail), text messaging, and online chat rooms.

6. Jean is on the deck of the *President Taft.* She seems content and is expecting a ship's crewmate to bring her a cup of beef tea. In predicting Jean's return to America, encourage students to refer back to evidence from the text. For example: "Jean will want to send a telegram to her grandmother since throughout the book, she has had written communication with her."

Teacher Notes:

Chapter Six

Name_____ Date_____ Class Period_____

Word List for Chapter Six

Character List:	Place Names, Proper Names, Terms, and Geography:
Jean's Father (Arthur) & Mother (Myrtle)	Pacific Ocean
	San Francisco
Andrea Hull	International Date Line
	Hawaiian Islands
David Hull	Honolulu
	Golden Gate Bridge
Aunt Kay	John Gilbert (American film actor)
	Charles Lindbergh
Jean's Grandmother and Grandfather	Mojave Desert
	Texas
Aunt Margaret	Ozark Mountains
	West Virginia

Vocabulary Words:

Requited (adj.)_____

Condemned (adj.)_____

Pigheaded (adj.)_____

Careen (v.)_____

Name_____ Date_____ Class Period_____

Geography Activity for Chapter Six

Track Jean's Journey Home:

Jean and her family travel from San Francisco to Washington, Pennsylvania by car. As you read this chapter, use a pencil and trace Jean and her family's route across the country. Locate and mark important locations and stops Jean makes along the way.

List of Places:

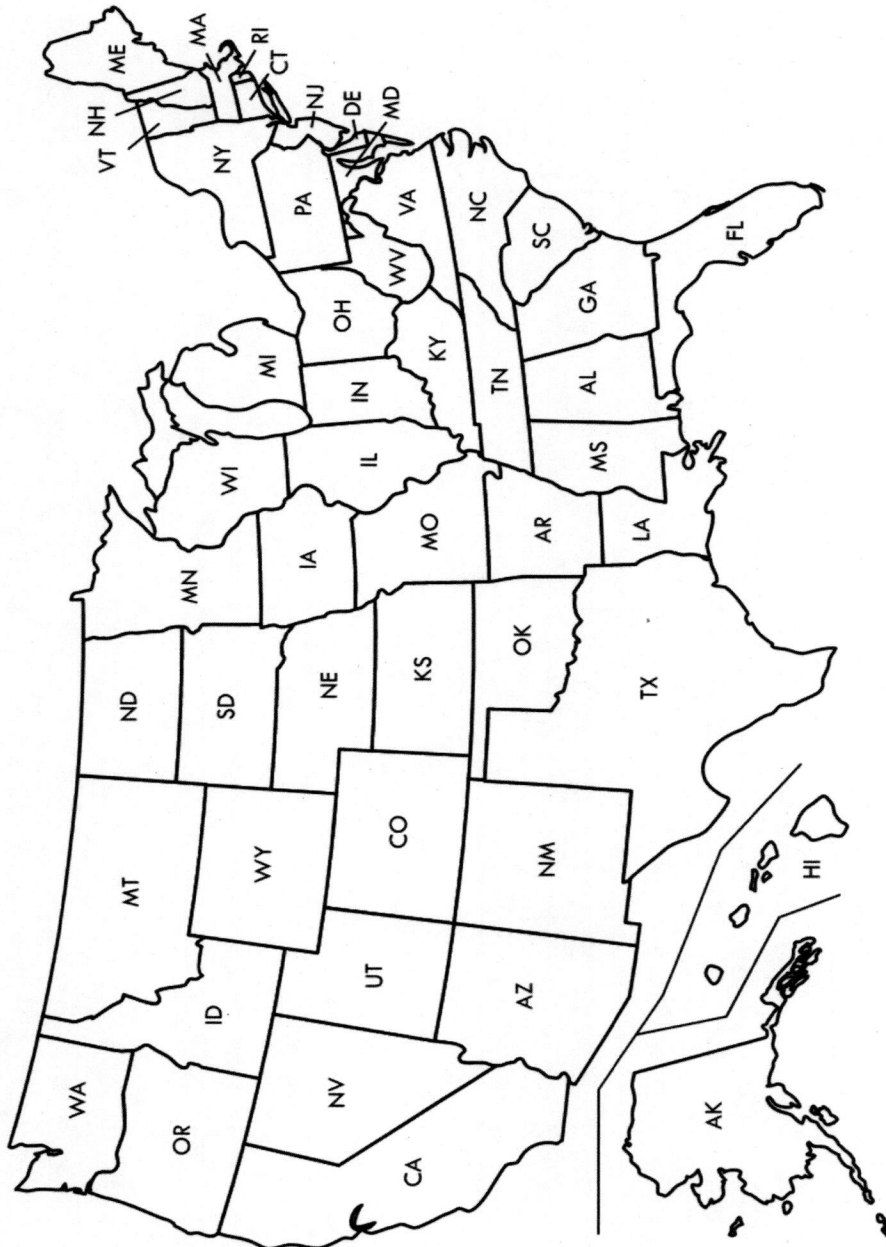

Reading Comprehension Questions for Chapter Six

1. How long is the journey from Shanghai to San Francisco by boat?

_____Pg # _____

2. What does Andrea notice about the passengers on the *President Taft?* Why is she disappointed?

_____Pg # _____

3. What is Jean's "'in-between' feeling"? What helps her to feel better?

_____

_____Pg # _____

4. What is the international date line?

_____

_____Pg # _____

5. What island does the ship stop at for a couple of days?

_____Pg # _____

6. At what point on her journey does Jean feel she will finally be able to say she has arrived in America?

_____Pg # _____

7. What do the U.S. inspectors do to ensure incoming passengers are safe to enter into the country?

_____

_____Pg # _____

8. How does Jean's family plan to travel from California to Pennsylvania?

_____

_____Pg # _____

9. What "narrow squeak" does Jean's father almost nearly not avoid? Why does this incident anger Jean?

_____

_____Pg # _____

10. Because of the rain, what obstacle almost prevents the car from driving up to Jean's grandparents' house? Why is this ironic?

_____

_____Pg # _____

Notes:

_____

_____

Discussion Questions for Chapter Six

1. What is Jean's definition of *belonging?* Do you agree?

2. Jean desperately wants to feel American. How does this cause an internal conflict for her?

3. Jean tells Andrea that she will feel truly American once she is in an American school, sings American songs, and participates in activities that other Americans do. How does Jean's conception of "being American" compare with your own idea of being American? Why do you suppose Jean has this particular notion?

4. How does the author impress on the reader the vastness of the United States?

5. Jean struggles with the feeling of "being in-between". She seems to characterize it as a negative trait that she feels coming home will help to cure her. However, what are ways in which being "in-between" is a positive trait. What are ways in which Jean can find healthy means to identify both as being an "American who grew up in China" and an American?

6. Will Jean's fantasy of being American match reality once she arrives in Washington, P.A.? Why or why not? Use evidence from the text to match your predictions.

Discussion Notes:
_____
_____
_____

Answer Key for Chapter 6 Reading Comprehension Questions

1. It takes 28 days for the President *Taft* to travel from Shanghai to San Francisco across the Pacific Ocean. **Pg. # 124**

2. Andrea notices that besides Jean, no kids their age are on board the ship. She is disappointed that there are no boys her age to talk about and flirt with on board the ship. Jean does not seem to share the same sentiments about boys as does Andrea. *N.B. Students might also point out the many different types of people that Jean notices populate the ship.* **Pgs. # 124-125**

3. She marvels on how being surrounded by the ocean makes her feel like she is in the middle of no place in particular. At night Jean looks at the stars and marvels how each star has its place. And once they pass the international date-line Jean feels further away from Lin Nai-Nai and China and closer to America. **Pgs. # 125; 126-127**

4. It is an imaginary line created to keep timetables in sync with the rotation of the earth. As ships sail from east to west in the Pacific Ocean, one "adds a day," and going west to east, one "drops a day". Also — the international date line is symbolic for Jean — for it helps her to manage her feelings of "being in-between". Jean imagines Lin Nai Nai on the other side of the planet after crossing the line. But once over the line, she feels like she is sharing the day with her grandmother. **Pgs. # 127-128**

5. They stop at the Hawaiian Islands (specifically, the port of Honolulu). **Pg. # 128**

6. Jean says she will feel as if she has arrived in America once the ship sails under the Golden Gate Bridge in San Francisco Bay. **Pg. # 131**

7. Passengers must prove their citizenship; Allow their luggage to be checked for illegal substances and they must undergo a health inspection to check for smallpox and other contagious diseases. **Pg. # 131**

8. Jean's father buys a brand new Dodge car that is waiting for him in San Francisco. They plan to drive the car across the country to Pennsylvania. **Pg. # 132**

9. They leave the main highway and take a shortcut that brings them to a condemned bridge. Jean's father ignores the warning sign posted on the bridge and drives the Dodge over the bridge anyway, despite Jean and her mother's protestations. It angers Jean because her father was stubborn. However, Jean does not like that she feels this way towards her father. **Pg. # 134-135**

10. It is ironic that the family has driven across the country to arrive home, but a rainstorm causes a mud puddle to form on the avenue leading to Jean's grandparents house. After all of the exploits, dangers, and obstacles that the family has faced, one mud puddle is all that stands between them and home. It is an irony that both Jean and her mother take note of. **Pg. # 137-138**

Teacher's Notes:

Discussion Questions Chapter 6 Answer Key

1. Answers will vary. With this question, it is crucial to have students first think about what Jean means by belonging. Remind students that Jean remarks that she felt as if "she was smack in the middle of no place ... Not in China, not in America, not in the past, not in the future." (p.125). Go further with students on this question and have them interrogate Jean's definition of belonging as it evolves throughout the novel. Jean did not feel like she belonged in China because there wasn't an institution that mimicked American values. But is that what she really needed to feel like she belonged?

2. Answers will vary. Help students to think about the difference between an external conflict and an internal one. The novel is complete with many examples of external conflicts (e.g., how her father pays off the coolies to avoid violence, how Jean deals with her British school teacher's insistence that she sing the anthem, escaping the war in Hankow, and so on). For internal conflict, consider Jean's self-concept. Her battle has to do with her identity. Jean has created an idealized version of what America will be for her. Is it a realistic one? How does this cause her to feel like she does not belong?

3. Answers will vary. This question puts pressure on what exactly Jean means by being American. Does Jean's conception of Americanness square with what your students think? Invite students to think critically about this issue, primarily as it deals with what we mean by shared communal values. Is there something that Americans share in common that makes one American? An honest discussion of this topic should reveal the diversity of

values and traditions that make up being American.

4. Answers will vary. This question ties nicely with the geography extension activity included in this lesson. Students who have not traveled extensively might not appreciate how far a distance it is to travel between San Francisco and Washington, P.A. Show students a map of the United States. Use an online map to calculate various distances.

5. Answers will vary. Again, this question deals with the theme of identity. Students who have never lived in another place other than the one in which they were born might have difficulty understanding this feeling of being in-between. Examples could include: speaking one language at home and another language at school; having citizenship that is different than that of your parents; living with two parents (because of divorce); having one parent who is of a different religion than the other).

6. Answers will vary. But teachers should know that in Chapter Seven, Jean will encounter racism and prejudice from her American classmates that surprise and stun her. In this vein, push students to think about how Jean's rose-tinted view may not be completely accurate.

Teacher Notes:

Geography Extension Activity Chapter Six Answer Key

Name **Answer Key** Date **1905** Class Period **First**

Geography Activity for Chapter 6 - *Homesick: My Own Story* by Jean Fritz

Track Jean's Journey Home:

Jean and her family travel from San Francisco to Washington, Pennsylvania by car. As you read this chapter, use a pencil and trace Jean and her family's route across the country. Locate and mark important locations and stops she makes along the way.

List of Places:
San Fransico
Honolulu
Ozarks
Texas
West Virginia
Pennsylvania

(map of the United States with handwritten annotations: "Washington, P.A.", "Virginia", "West Virginia", "The Ozarks", "Long Flat stretches of Texas", "Note: The ship stops in Honolulu for several days", "Travel see", "Mojave Desert", "San Francisco", "To china")

Chapter Seven

Characters and Geography List for Chapter 7

Character List:	**Geography:**

Character List:

Aunt Margaret

Grandmother

Grandfather

Miss Crofts

Aunt Blanche, Aunt Etta, Aunt Mary L., Aunt Sarah

Uncle Welsh, Uncle George, Aunt Edith

Elizabeth, Jane, Katherine, Charlotte

Ruth and Marie

Andrew Carr

Donald Burch

Geography:

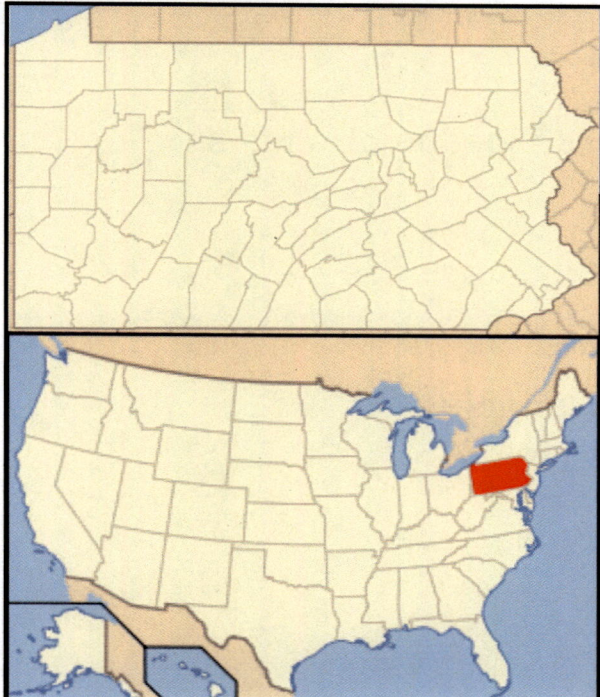

Jean's family lives in Washington, Pennsylvania. Locate and label the approximate location of Washington on the state map above. Label the state of Pennsylvania on the United States map below.

Image Credit: Wikimedia Commons

Name_____ Date_____ Class Period_____

Phrases, Unique Terms, and Idioms:

"Nide muchin shr ega da wukwei"	*The Palmer Method*
The Pledge of Allegiance	Copycats
Silk stockings	"It was a flop"
Flannel cakes	Cooties
Smearcase	Chrysanthemums
Gingham dress	

Vocabulary Words:

ruffle (v.)_____	spasm (n.)_____
shelling (v. phrase)_____	silo (n.)_____
daintily (adv.)_____	commotion (n.)_____
meek (adj.)_____	sly (adj._____

Name_____ Date_____ Class Period_____

Reading Comprehension Questions for Chapter 7

1. What emotions does Jean have about the family farm when she first arrives in Washington, P.A.?

_____

_____Pg # _____

2. Why doesn't Aunt Margaret name the chickens?

_____Pg #_____

3. Why does Jean think Ruth and Marie are ignorant? What's Aunt Margaret's explanation?

_____

_____Pg # _____

4. What is Jean's grandmother's theory about writers?

_____Pg # _____

5. What grade will Jean start in the Fall?

_____Pg # _____

6. What is the name of Jean's new teacher in America?

_____Pg # _____

7. How does Andrew Car insult Jean in class? What does Jean do in response?

_____Pg # _____

8. What does Jean picture in her mind as she recites the Pledge of Allegiance?

_____Pg # _____

9. What is the Palmer Method?

_____

_____Pg #_____

10.   After Jean's first day of school, how does Jean's grandmother help her to feel better?

_____

_____Pg #_____

Notes:

_____

_____

_____

_____

Discussion Questions for Chapter 7

1. What were Jean's expectations for what life in America would be like? What are some aspects that feel familiar for her? What is a surprise? Can you relate to Jean's experiences?

2. How are American represented in this chapter?

3. Jean encounters stereotypes about Asian people when she arrives in Pennsylvania. How does Jean respond? What would you do if you were Jean and someone said something derogatory about another race or ethnicity?

4. Jean has conflicts with both her teacher in China and her new teacher in America. What do these conflicts say about Jean? Why do you think she has problems with authority?

5. Is Jean happy at the end of the novel? Why or why not?

Notes:

_____

_____

_____

_____

_____

Answer Key for Chapter 7 Reading Comprehension Questions

1. Jean feels like everything is familiar to her and she doesn't "need to be told what to do". **Pg. # 139**

2. Aunt Margaret doesn't want to become too attached to the chickens since all the animals on the farm are eventually used as food and eaten! **Pg. # 140**

3. Ruth and Marie ask Jean if in China people eat rats and rats' tails, snakes, and so on. They incorrectly call chopsticks "sticks". Jean is taken aback by the questions and the lack of understanding from her peers. Aunt Margaret explains that "Some people in Washington don't know any better," and for people in America, China is a far-away place so people "imagine strange things". **Pg. # 142; 143**

4. Jean's grandmother says writers don't always "fit in". **Pg. # 147**

5. Jean starts Eighth Grade. **Pg. # 143**

6. The name of Jean's new teacher in America is Miss Crofts. **Pg. # 148**

7. Andrew Car uses a derogatory slur for Chinese people. Jean stands up and says, "You call them *Chinese.*" She corrects her classmates and they are surprised and silenced and the teacher intervenes. **Pg. # 149**

8. Jean pictures in her mind the flag raised and waving on the Bund in Hankow as she says the Pledge of Allegiance. **Pg. # 150**

9. The Palmer Method is a handwriting style that Jean's teacher makes her learn. Later, Jean finds out that all children in America learn this method. It causes letters to appear slanted and students have to learn to write with their wrists and not move their hands when writing. She does not like the new method and argues that her penmanship is fine just the way it is. **Pgs. # 154-155**

10. She commiserates with Jean and agrees with her that the Palmer Method is not an ideal way to learn to write letters. The two pick grapes and Jean's grandmother makes Apple dumplings. **Pgs. # 158-159**

Teacher Guide for Chapter Seven Discussion Questions

1. Answers will vary. Students search for evidence in the text to back-up their answers.

2. Answers will vary. Students search for evidence in the text to back up their answers.

3. First, discuss stereotypes. Explain that stereotypes are generalizations people make about others. While a stereotype can sometimes be based in fact, one makes an assumption when they apply the stereotype to all individuals within that group. It is a stereotype that smart people wear glasses. This stereotype arises because we associate glasses with reading and people who read are perceived as smarter. But not every "smart person" wears glasses and not everyone who wears glasses is smart.

4. Refer back to Jean's relationship with her teacher at the British school in Hankow. She was made to sing the British national anthem (which she protested against by merely mouthing the words). In America, Jean does not agree with her school's new writing method. So she slightly rebels. Jean is a person who does not believe in something just because an authority says so. She has a bit of her father's stubbornness and her mother's practical sense. It seems as a healthy bit of rebellion runs in the family as even Jean's grandmother takes her side.

5. Answers will vary.

Teacher's Notes

Suggested Unit Plan for *Homesick: My Own Story* by Jean Fritz (Pre-Reading, Chapters 1-7)

Essential Question: How do I thrive in a world where I feel I don't belong?

Time Duration: 45-minute lesson sessions

Historical Time Period: 1920s in Hankow, China - The Republic of China and the Nationalist Rebellion in China

Primary Source: *Homesick: My Own Story* by Jean Fritz

Chapter One Lesson

Day One - Pre-Reading Activity

1. Write the essential question on the board: How do I thrive in a world where I feel I don't belong?
   a. Students can share out answers or they can complete a 3-minute do-now.

- Provide every student with a copy of the book *Homesick: My Own Story* by Jean Fritz.
   a. What do students notice about the cover of the book?
   b. You can mention that the novel is a Newbery Honor book, which means it was selected as one of the best books written for children and young people. You can take some time and talk about the Newbery Award and ask students if they know any other Newbery Medal winning books?

- Write the word autobiography so everyone in the class can see it. Explain to students that *Homesick* is based on the events of a real person, Jean Fritz, the author. However, she tells her own story without bothering about putting all the events in the right order.
   a. Display on the board the following sentence: The author's fictionalized version, though all the events are

true, of her childhood in China in the 1920s.

    b. You can mention that this sentence comes from the Library of Congress Cataloging-in-Publication data in the front of the book.

    c. Ask students to think about whether you can tell a fictional story about real events?

    d. Have students look over the Foreword to the book. Give students a few moments to look at the Foreword with a partner. What is Jean Fritz's explanation that her book is both fictional and true?

- Have students give you the gist of Jean Fritz's explanation. They can write this down in their notebooks.
- Display this information: "October 1925 to September 1927"

    a. Distribute a timeline to students (A simple Google search will suffice to find a generic timeline). It is sometimes helpful for students to get a sense of the time period. Add the current month and year to the timeline. Add two other important dates to the timeline to give context.

    b. Explain to students this is the timeline of events in the novel they'll be reading with you. You can tell students that they are not required to know the exact dates of events because Jean Fritz's novel reads like a story and not like a history book.

- This is a great opportunity to elicit from students their background knowledge about China. What do they know? You can use a KWL chart to do this activity but I find just having students share out what they know will tell you a lot about your students' understanding of Asia and its history.

    a. Students should know the location of the following locations on a map of China:

        i.   Beijing (the capital)

        ii. Yellow River

      iii.   Yangtze River

      iv.   Shanghai

      v.   Hankow (sometimes spelled Hankou). The modern name is Wuhan.

  b. Display a map of China on the smartboard or distribute copies of a map of China to every student.

  c. Guide students to identify the places on the map.

- Homework: Have students complete any work on the timeline or on the map that is not completed. Also - I would give students a folder or some sort of organizational device so they can keep all of their handouts in one place.

Day Two - Pre-Reading Activity II

1. Explain to students that before we jump into the novel we are going to examine a primary source image.

2. Entrance Ticket - Distribute copies to every student of figure 1 - the Chinese Junk. Students should work independently at first to locate details in the picture.

3. Read the description out loud of the ship. Guide students to find other details in the picture. Have students share with a partner.

4. Circulate the room and after a few minutes guide students to identify details they did not notice.

5. Explain to students that they will read the first page of the novel together as a class. Start with the first page and end with the sentence "In America with my Grandmother".

  a. As you read, point out the Yangtze River. Ask students what does Jean notice when she observes the river.

  b. After reading the first page, answer the first questions (1-3) together with your class. Using a document camera helps with this activity. Model for students how you would paraphrase answers and make note of the page numbers you found the correct answer.

6. Homework: Handout out the word list. For homework have

students complete the entries for the following words and terms: Characters: Jean, Jean's Father. Geography: Hankow, Yangtze River. For the vocabulary word list starting with "Globe" have students paraphrase a definition.

There are several ways you can conduct the reading of Chapter 1. You can have students read the entire chapter for homework. This may work for a more advanced class - or you can read Chapter 1 together as a class. I recommend taking the time to read Chapter 1 together as a class and guiding them through the answering of the comprehension questions so in later chapters students will feel more confident in completing this task.

Day Three - Chapter 1
1. There are several ways you can read Chapter 1. Choose what is right for your class. However you do it - have students complete all of the reading comprehension questions.
2. If you do not finish chapter 1 in class - it is perfectly fine - assign the rest of the chapter for homework and tell students to be prepared for a discussion of Chapter One.

Day Four - Chapter 1
1. Do the first three discussion questions together as a class.
2. Spice it up and have the students work together in groups to complete the remaining questions. I recommend you inform students that they will be evaluated on their group work performance.
3. Homework: Read Chapter 2 (see my lesson for Chapter 2).

Chapter Two Lesson
Day Five
1. For Homework students should have read Chapter 2.
2. Write / Keep the essential question on the board: How do I

thrive in a world where I feel I don't belong?

    a. Provide every student with a copy of the book *Homesick: My Own Story* by Jean Fritz.

2. Do now / warm up - When was a time you felt homesick?
3. For reading comprehension questions 1-6, use the document camera to model how you would find the answer to these questions. If your students need the extra practice, read pages 30-31 aloud and check for understanding.
4. Talk about Jean's letter to her grandmother on page 31. Also see discussion question #2. How does Jean show signs of homesickness?
5. For the rest of the class have students work in group to complete the remaining comprehension questions.
6. Homework: Word List worksheet for Chapter 2

Day Six -

1. Do Now - Have your reading comprehension questions out and ready to discuss.
2. Popcorn the class and ask them some of the reading comprehension questions.
3. Make sure students have the gist of all the major plot points.
4. For the Discussion questions for this chapter, it is important that the teacher at least explain some of the historical dynamics that are going on in China during this time - especially as it relates to how Jean and Andrea witness the rebellious Chinese farmers and Jean Fritz's explanation of the rising rebellion. Use the graphic organizer at the end of the discussion question worksheet to give notes to your students (or have them research and discuss).
5. Use the remaining discussion questions for small group work.

    a. However, question #1 is a great question for large group discussion.

6. Homework: Complete word list worksheet.

Days Seven and Eight

1. Use these days to wrap up Chapter 2 and to do the extension activities with your students - it is also a good idea to do some research with your students. Have your students locate websites that are reputable and accurate about life in China during the 1920s. Provide students with an online research tracker. You may want to circulate the room and once students have found good resources give them the research tracker and instruct them to record essential information about the website (the URL, the source, reliability, and so on). In addition, have students find maps of Hankow that date to the time Jean lived in the city. This is a good time for students to look more closely at the photographs at the end of the book - especially the Hull's house and Lin Nai Nai; the pictures of the Bund, the Chinese junk, and so on. How are the actual pictures different (or the same from what you imagined in your mind)?
2. Homework: Read Chapter 3

Chapter Three Lesson

Day Nine

1. Do now. What is a revolution? Based on what we've read so far how is China changing its government?
2. Students work in groups to complete the Word List for Chapter 3.
3. If your students have already read the chapter then you can guide them through the comprehension questions; or, alternatively, you can read the chapter as a class, stopping where appropriate.
4. HW: complete Word List and Reading Comprehension Questions for Ch. 3

Day Ten -
   1. Dedicate a day for a web quest and have your students complete the Extension Activity that is attached to the comprehension worksheet.
   2. You will need to give your students access to the internet and a device to be able to complete the web quest.

Day Eleven
   1. Use the discussion questions to lead your class into a conversation about the contents of this chapter. The theme of Chapter 3 is loss. Some of the content is heavy. A child dies. Jean and her family have to deal with grief.
   2. Use the double entry journal (see attached) as an exit ticket.
   3. Homework: Read Chapter 4.

Chapter Four Lesson

Essential Question: How would you live through a siege?
Historical Time Period: 1920s in Hankou, China - The Republic of China and the Chinese Civil War (different factions in China vie for power in the newfound Republic)
Primary Source: *Homesick: My Own Story* by Jean Fritz
Grade Level: Ideal for Middle School grades (6, 7, and 8). For EFLs - any grade.

Day 12
   1. **Do now.** What is a siege?
   2. Display the word list on a projector or SmartBoard. Guide students to think about some of the more difficult words or unique words. Point out that the word "giddyap" is an onomatopoeia. As a class, define the word "siege". Note that a synonym for a siege is "blockade".
   3. Students work in groups to complete the Word List for Chapter 3.
   4. If your students have already read the chapter then you can

guide them through the comprehension questions; or, alternatively, you can read the chapter as a class, stopping where appropriate.

5. HW: complete Word List and Reading Comprehension Questions for Ch. 3

Day 13 & 14

1. Cold call students on random reading comprehension questions.

2. Use the discussion questions to lead your class into a conversation about the contents of this chapter. The theme of Chapter 3 is division. Some of the content is heavy. Jean and her family still deal with the grief of the loss of Mirriam.

3. I highly recommend to use the discussion questions as a way to have students write about the chapter. Students can choose a question and go further in a short written response.

Chapter Five Lesson

Essential Question: What is the best way to say goodbye?
Historical Time Period: 1920s in Hankou, China - The Republic of China and the Chinese Civil War (different political factions in China vie for power in the newfound Republic)
Primary Source: *Homesick: My Own Story* by Jean Fritz
Grade Level: Ideal for Middle School grades. For EFLs - any grade.

Day 15 -

1. Do now. Respond to the prompt: What is it like to say goodbye?

2. Students work in groups to complete the Word List for Chapter 5.

3. If your students have already read the chapter then you can guide them through the comprehension questions; or,

alternatively, you can read the chapter as a class, stopping where appropriate.

4. Exit Ticket: 3-2-1 (Three things I learned today, two things I wonder about; and one question I have).
5. HW: complete Word List and Reading Comprehension Questions for Ch. 5

Day 16 -

1. Cold call students to answer random reading comprehension questions.
2. Use the discussion questions to lead your class into a conversation about the contents of this chapter. The theme of Chapter 5 is the difficulty in saying goodbye.
3. Writing Activity: Choose one of the discussion questions as a writing prompt.
4. Homework: Read Chapter 6.

Day 17 -

Extension Activity: The chapter includes references to cablegrams, the Victrola, and the Charleston. Have students go deeper into the history and cultural significance of these innovations in arts and science. Students research and compile a list of interesting websites and books related to one or all.

Chapter Six Lesson

Essential Question: What does it mean to belong to a country?
Historical Time Period: 1920s in Hankou, China - The Republic of China and the Chinese Civil War (different political factions in China vie for power in the newfound Republic); 1920s America.
Primary Source: *Homesick: My Own Story* by Jean Fritz
Grade Level: Ideal for Middle School grades. For EFLs - any grade.

Day 18 -

1. Do now. Make a prediction. How will Jean feel she has truly arrived in America? Explain your answer.
2. Students work in groups to complete the Word List for Chapter 5. Alternatively, assign words or groups of words to individual students.
3. If your students have already read the chapter then you can guide them through the comprehension questions; or, alternatively, you can read the chapter as a class, stopping where appropriate.
4. Exit Ticket: Discuss your predictions.
5. HW: complete Word List and Reading Comprehension Questions for Ch. 6

Day 19 -
1. Cold call students to answer random reading comprehension questions (to check for understanding).
2. Use the discussion questions to lead your class into a conversation about the contents of this chapter. The theme of Chapter 6 is about identity, specifically how it becomes associated with nationality.
3. Writing Activity: Choose one of the discussion questions as a writing prompt.
4. Homework: Read Chapter 7.

Geography Extension Activity: Use the map provided to have students trace Jean and her family trip across the American continent. Students will need access to an atlas or a device with internet access to locate geographical places.

Chapter Seven Lesson

Essential Question: How do I belong to a community or group?
Historical Time Period: 1920s in Hankou, China - The Republic of China and the Chinese Civil War (different factions in China vie for power in the newfound Republic); 1920s America
Primary Source: *Homesick: My Own Story* by Jean Fritz

Day 20 -
1. **Do now.** What is America for Jean? For you? For us?
2. Teacher displays word lists on a projector and distributes copies to students. Students work in groups to complete the Word List for Chapter 7.
3. If your students have already read the chapter then you can guide them through the comprehension questions; or, alternatively, you can read the chapter as a class, stopping where appropriate.
4. **HW:** complete Word List and Reading Comprehension Questions for Ch. 7

Day 21 -
1. Cold Call students to answer random reading comprehension questions.
2. Use discussion questions as a means to assess students' understanding of the chapter.
3. Devote time to discussing stereotypes. Have students identify the stereotypes that show up in Chapter Seven. Use discussion as an exit ticket.

Go Digital: Google Forms Assessment Links for Each Chapter

Using This Assessment with Google Forms

Make a Copy	Google Form Links	Share Your Form
Use the persistent links I have provided to access a unique copy of the Google Form.	Homesick: My Own Story **Chapter One** https://bit.ly/3gdxfva **Chapter Two** https://bit.ly/3saAGcT **Chapter Three** https://bit.ly/3i0YtHO **Chapter Four** https://bit.ly/2K3szha **Chapter Five** https://bit.ly/3ozLO0W **Chapter Six** https://bit.ly/3i7KrnK **Chapter Seven** http://ow.ly/DpPw30rs3Oi	When you are ready to share your form on Google Classroom or by email or by sharing the student-facing link, click the button on the right hand-side of the form.
Google Drive Copy document Would you like to make a copy of ? Make a copy Google will ask you to make a copy of the form. Select "make a copy". You now have your own copy of this form that you can use with your students!		When students complete the assessment, you can review their answers. The form is set up to manually release answers so the teacher can read through each students' response and write additional feedback, if needed.

Note to users: Each of the above links is a persistent link to make a copy of the Google Form for your use and your use only. You will need a Google account to use these links and access to Google Forms.

Bibliography

American Library Association. "Welcome to the Newbery Medal Home Page!", American Library Association, November 30, 1999. <https://goo.gl/CevUUW>

China Blank Map, Blank Map of China Showing Yangtze River and Yellow River, China Travel Map. <http://www.chinamaps.org/china/china-blank-map-large-6.html>

Fritz, Jean. *Homesick: My Own Story*. Puffin. 1982.

"Keying (Ship)." *Wikipedia*, Wikimedia Foundation, 31 Oct. 2018, <en.wikipedia.org/wiki/Keying_(ship)>.

"K-W-L Chart." *ReadWriteThink*, National Council of Teachers of English. <www.readwritethink.org/files/resources/printouts/KWL%20Chart.pdf>.

Scott, Walter, William V. Moody, and Mary R. Willard. *The Lay of the Last Minstrel*. Chicago: Scott, Foresman, 1899. Print. <https://books.google.com/books?id=7oIAAAAYAAJ&>

Timeline. Education Place. <https://www.eduplace.com/graphicorganizer/pdf/timeline.pdf>

Appendix

Peer Speaking & Listening Evaluation Form

Suggestions on the Use of the Speaking & Listening Evaluation Form: There are two ways to use this peer evaluation form:

- Model for students how you want them to use the evaluation form. Project a copy of the form with a document camera and illustrate what you would do when filling out the form.
  - For example, use a think-a-aloud process. Say, "Can I provide evidence for each of the bullet points on this form? When I put a check next to a standard, what does that mean? If I put an X next to a standard, what does that mean? If I put a question mark next to a standard, what does that mean?
- You can also use other annotation marks for students to use, such as a linear scale of 1 to 5, or 1 to 4, or something similar.
  - Adding a scale helps older students who may see granularity in their performance. Giving oneself a two rather than a one indicates that they were not completely off the mark while acknowledging that they could do better.
- Make a copy and give it to your students after they complete discussion questions or at the end of a class period where students are speaking and listening.
- First, students evaluate themselves. It's a simple way to keep students accountable and, if used often, establishes a routine that formalizes the speaking and listening standards in your classroom.
- Second, students evaluate their group by filling out the second column. Students can add the names of students in their group to the form.
  - Alternatively, use this second column for presentations or when kids speak to the whole class at once. Tip: You can cut the sheet in half and use it as a half sheet to avoid confusion.

How Did They Do?

Name _____

Directions: Complete the following peer review task tracker.

- ☐ Student initiates and participates effectively in a range of collaborative discussions.
- ☐ Student builds on others' ideas and express their own clearly and persuasively.
- ☐ Student responds thoughtfully to diverse perspectives.
- ☐ Student summarizes points of agreement and disagreement.
- ☐ Students can, when needed, qualify or justify others' viewpoints and understandings.
- ☐ Student makes new connections in light of the evidence and reasoning presented.
- ☐ Student integrate and evaluate information presented in diverse ways.

How Did I Do?

Name _____

Directions: Assess your work by completing the following task tracker.

- ☐ I initiate and participate effectively in a range of collaborative discussions.
- ☐ I build on others' ideas and express my own clearly and persuasively.
- ☐ I respond thoughtfully to diverse perspectives.
- ☐ I summarize points of agreement and disagreement.
- ☐ I can, when needed, qualify or justify others' viewpoints and understandings.
- ☐ I make new connections in light of the evidence and reasoning presented.
- ☐ I integrate and evaluate information presented in diverse ways.

Frayer Model for Vocabulary Instruction

How To Use This Resource: Use Frayer models to teach vocabulary in context related to your class reading of Jean Fritz's novel *Homesick: My Own Story*. When working with a text where an unfamiliar word appears, assign the Frayer Model template. First, you model for students what you want them to do with the explanatory model and the student sample. Choose a simple word and complete a Frayer model in class with your students.

Students have to think dynamically in order to complete a Frayer model. For **the meaning section** ensure students are putting the definition into their own words; For **the characteristics section**, it's best to have students think about what this word "looks like". How is the word used? **For example**, students can rely on connections. Have students research the word. How is it used, and in what field? **Non-examples** are a fun section because the answer does not come quickly. It's okay to see students get frustrated with this model. But the work pays off.

Use the sketch section in two ways. Print out these sets and have students illustrate this section — label an example. Alternatively, use the editable version of this resource and have students insert .jpgs or .pngs to create an illustration. Find the editable version here: Make sure you are logged into a Google Account. Choose "make a copy". **https://bit.ly/3dDljov**

How to Create a Frayer Model

The Frayer Method to Learn Vocabulary

Meaning
DON'T COPY AND PASTE. FIRST LOOK UP THE WORD IN MORE THAN ONE DICTIONARY. DISTILL THE MEANING OF THE WORD. TRY TO EXPLAIN THE WORD TO SOMEONE WHO DOES NOT UNDERSTAND. ULTIMATELY PUT THE MEANING IN YOUR OWN WORDS!

Characteristics
LIST THE ESSENTIAL ASPECTS OF WHAT MAKES WHAT YOU ARE DEFINING WHAT IT IS. THINK ABOUT WHAT PARTS MAKE UP THE WHOLE. FOR EXAMPLE, YOU CANNOT HAVE MYTH WITHOUT ORAL STORYTELLING OR TRADITION. OR, YOU CANNOT HAVE A CAR WITHOUT AN IGNITION.

Examples
FIND WHERE YOUR WORD OR TERM EXISTS IN REAL LIFE. IF IT HAD A RESIDENCE WHERE WOULD IT LIVE? FIND A SENTENCE. YOU CAN GIVE TITLE OF BOOKS OR MOVIES, ALLUSIONS TO LITERATURE. EXAMPLES FROM YOUR OWN OTHERS' LIVES, OR WHEREVER YOU MAY HAVE FOUND YOUR TERM.

Non-examples
SOLIDIFY YOUR UNDERSTANDING BY LISTING WHAT YOUR TERM OR WORD IS NOT. FOR EXAMPLE, A MYTH IS NOT A NOVEL OR NONFICTION. LIST ALTERNATIVELY, MISCONCEPTIONS ABOUT YOUR TERM OR WORD. HOW IS IT CONFUSED WITH SIMILAR BUT DIFFERENT IDEAS OR CONCEPTS?

Sketch
Label Your Sketch

Use a camera and create your own image.

Draw.
Sketch.
Doodle.

Your Sketch
Your Doodle
Your Image
Symbols
Diagrams

Find quality images online that make your word POP!

Use words and images

Frayer Model Vocabulary

Name _____

Your Term: _____

Meaning	Characteristics
Examples	**Non-examples**

Sketch

Title of Text: _____

Page Number of text word is used: _____

Student Example Frayer Model Vocabulary
Myth (*noun*)

Meaning	Characteristics
- Ancient oral tale - Old story - A story with insight into humanity - A belief that is possibly not true but people believe it - Urban Legend - A creature or animal that is fantastic or extinct (e.g., the myth of the unicorn)	- Often oral and not written - Passed down from generation to generation - Every culture and historical period has their own set of myths - Myth are shared by people and form a sense of group identity - Myths are typically short and easily told

Examples	Non-examples
- Ancient Greek myths often were oral tales - The myth of Sisyphus is a myth because it happened a long time ago and it exists in the oral tradition	- Non-fiction - Information texts - Primary source interview - Novel - Does a myth stay a myth once it is recorded and written down.

Sketch

Myths are linked together and tell us something about a culture

Title of Text: *Parallel Myth by J.F. Bierlein*

Page Number of text word is used: p.17

Think About Any Quote!

Your Quote: _____ Name: _____

When I think of this quote the following inferences comes to my mind:

1.	4.
2.	5.
3.	6.

Your Quote: _____ Name: _____

When I rewrite this quote in my own words it most nearly means:

3-Box Note-taking Template

Name:

Class:

Date:

Topic: *Homesick*

Notes:

Questions:

Summary:

Cornell Note-taking Template

Name: _____ Class: _____

Topic: _____ Date:_____

Cues	Notes

Summary:

You have just read a Teacher's Guide and Novel Study for Jean Fritz's Homesick:

My Own Story

by Greig Roselli

Things you can do after reading this book!

- **Take a moment and write a review on Amazon. Other readers will be interested in what you have to say, and it only takes a few moments.**

- **Check out Greig Roselli's blog Stones of Erasmus (www.stonesoferasmus.com). It's chock full of good writing, ideas, inspiration, and teacher-inspired-fun.**

- **Give the book to a friend or donate to a library and keep the sharing going**

I see ya 😊

About the Author: Greig Roselli is a ten-year veteran teacher. Born in South Louisiana, he currently lives and works in New York City. You can contact him via email at greigroselli@stonesoferasmus.com or on his website - stonesoferasmus.com.

Other Books by Greig Roselli:

- *Philosophy in the Classroom: Lessons on Philosophy with Young People*
- *Things I Probably Shouldn't Have Said and Other Faux Pas*
- *We Was Talking Pretty and Scribbling in the Snow*

Made in the USA
Middletown, DE
25 July 2022